The Black Titan Group

Do we not come from the spirit of
the ancient visions?

Are we not the culture for every advance
humanity, builders of lasting civilizations

"When In The Black"

ISBN 13: 9780692055212
ISBN 10: 0692055215

Acknowledgements (The Intelligent Life Source that encouraged me to write this book)

Published by The Black Titan Publication, Marietta, Georgia

"When In The Black"
The How To Book To Security
How To Achieve Your Mental Wealth

Table of Contents:

Chapter 1. How To Be Free From Mental Poverty.
Chapter 2. How To Define Security.
Chapter 3. How To Conquer The Red (Liabilities)
Chapter 4. How To Locate Directions In The Marketplace
Chapter 5. How To See Opportunities In Front Of You.
Chapter 6. How To Secure Your Master Mind Alliance.
Chapter 7. How To Learn From Successful Mentors.

Chapter 8. How To See Assets Over Liabilities.
Chapter 9. How To Overcome Negative Losses In Investing.
Chapter 10. How To Be Aware and Avoid Bad Company
Chapter 11. How To Partner With The Experts:
Chapter 12. How To Live When In The Black.

Foreword

When I was asked to write the foreword for this excellent book all I could do was smile at the growth of the seeds that I have planted over the years in the lives of many across the world. This wealth of information is a much needed time in our History. Black people of African descent all over the world suffer from Mental Poverty even if they financially rich. Everywhere I've visited in the world some other ethnicity on top and the black people are on the bottom in the social order of power. This is not by coincidence but by explicit design. This social engineering has made to date over two thousand Billionaires in the world, wherein only twelve are black and only three of African-American citizenship. We as a race group lag behind in building communities, commerce, businesses, and governments, and we suffer economically because we spend ninety-seven percent of our income (dollars) with by everyone else. Those who do have money in our black community do not invest back into the community they once lived in so the cycle of debts, liabilities, and poverty continues to plague us as a whole. It was decided over five hundred years ago that people of African descent would be socially engineered into the permanent underclassmen and now the base of consumerism while other race groups would be Merchants and Producers. We excel at preaching, singing, rapping, acting, dancing, athletics, but frown upon investing, starting new ventures, businesses, building (700-850) credit scores, supporting black owned enterprises, learning specialized skills, inventing new things, and stepping out of our comfort zone. This must change if we are to survive and thrive together in the 21st century and beyond. We must form strategic think tanks, by supporting organizations like, the Harvest Institute; the National Black Economic Network Organization; the United African Movement; We Buy The Block; and leverage our black philosophy, and manifest black thought without the fear of political correctness, we need investment clubs, credit unions, land banks, imports/exports, and agricultural science companies and more in order to become competitive in the Economical order of the world. We have done Religious order that's not working, we have done political order and that hasn't worked in our economic favor. Maybe it's time to do

Economics different and gain Real Black Wealth and Worth and Power. I salute you my Brother Daryl aka "Heru" for this taking on this incredible task of awakening our race to enter the race for Mental Wealth and Real Security. Asè.

Foreword by: Joseph Carswell
Founder and CEO of Capital Funding Partner, Inc.

Introduction:

An adopted black youth surviving in the lower income class of Americanism, when your birth parents (m.i.a); some would calculate those odds in favor of incarceration… But I defied stereotypical disadvantages in my neighborhood. I recall the first twenty-one years of my existence in a poor environment; but my mental environment never accepted such conditions, it was not a struggle in the since of the word for me, not like my Ancestors before me, on whom shoulders I owe my foundation too; yes I know and heard the stories of underpaid or never paid hard labor plantations, the reconstruction era and the jim crow inequalities, and all the other disadvantages, but nevertheless survival was the order of my days, months, and years to come for me; regardless of the odds stacked against me. Where most youths like me started out with what we were given to work with. So I survived the first portion of my life as my parents conditioned me to survive the encounters of Americanism; this portion of my life was not defined by me, and was not going to define me; it was my parents conditioning me to accept these mediocre conditions, because of their mental conditioning in the south; it was not my self determination yet. (sidebar) But I honor my mother who adopted me, she was my shining example of selflessness; and she invested in her family with the scarcity she could muscle up, with the little of what was earned by her enduring strength, sacrificing her own dreams and aspirations to care for her family needs, and a husband (my grandfather) with dementia, back in them days we called it *"senile"*, or *"old folk disease"*. We couldn't put our elders away in old folk homes, and shouldn't now; so we all pitch in to help my father. My mother woke up early to catch the bus to be off to work before five a.m. We were told she was going to work for the "white man over the mountain", the affluent side of the city of Birmingham, Alabama. We were told to call him "Mr. Johnson", he was a Shriner I recalled, a Businessman, he gave us tickets to the circus; my mom did what most black women did in those times, took care of "the white men homes" called a "mammy" (that's my real mother's first name) what a coincidence. She loved her boss and their kids as her own, one child became our childhood friend, my mother brought us his kids "*Hand Me Downs*", I thought kindly of the things he gave us, they were good things to me. Some things were new and some were used; like shoes, clothing, school books, etc. You know the rest of the black story. We were told he was a good man, and to respect his generosity, and we did. We had many things other kids didn't have back then, and we had to share, even though silently we fought over who would wear what first, but my mom were right about Mr. Johnson, when he passed away, he left in his (**Will**) the wishes to give my mother a home in Norwood, a once all white neighborhood in Birmingham that was desegregated in the early seventies. I attended the first integrated classes at Norwood Elementary. Mr. Johnson rewarded my mom with a house too big to up keep after each passing years, we couldn't maintain that house, and the amenities there, maintenance became too much to handle, it was *above our means* at the time, with very little income coming in and all the bills to pay, it was not possible to keep the roof from sinking in on us, therefore whenever it rained, it leaked in the house and we had to put out the foot tubs and buckets, and whatever else we could find to catch the water when it rain too hard and long, it was too big to keep warm as well, had heavy quilts up to keep certain rooms warm to sleep in, to keep cold air out; for she didn't have much money or the help to fix such a steep pitch roof, we eventually had to move to the project in Ensley, Alabama when I became eight years old. We were on a waiting list for years for a large enough housing to accommodate seven people, plus all the people who were not on the lease staying overnight, she could've gotten put out for having them there; but eventually she was known with "the housing authority" as a caring woman, she was affectionately called "Mama Hen" because she loved helping people. She said be thankful always, it could be worse. She said remember the house that was given to us for my loving, loyal, faithful service as a maid. She believed in "*reaping what you sow*". This very grateful attitude I accepted as a youth, because of other's charity. But I was not satisfied with such meagerness at all, so I discovered my many gifts I could apply to help my mother. The first one, was learning, I was an excellent student, recommended by the teachers to be skipped twice as a youth, but my mother insisted I stay behind, so I wouldn't out perform my siblings at learning, didn't want them to feel some type of way she said, but instead she asked me to help them with their homework, and she made sure I help them with their homework. Sure I felt some type of way, but nevertheless I helped, because I loved my siblings, and didn't want them to fail either, My Second gift was drawing, as early as seven, got accepted at thirteen years of age to a fine art school for my impressive drawings, but couldn't go, no family lived in Atlanta to see after me away from home, now around that same time, I discovered my ability to cut hair at ten, and became good enough to earn three dollars per cut. Then around twelve years of age I went up to five dollars; after that I became great at cutting hair; I were cutting hair on the front porch, back porch, in the kitchen, anywhere in the neighborhood until around seventeen. Now, at that age I was charging eight dollars. Around this time I stop excelling in the classroom by choice, went to a school I didn't choose, did just enough to get by, went to summer school, and night school, just to acquire enough credits for my diploma. I did want to go to college or barbering school because my reputation got out about my skills, I began to have too many customers in and around my mother's project apartment, the neighborhood cops were my customers as well. I began seeking a barber shop to work in, came to work with three women who made space for me in a very tiny shop, called Golden Rules Barber Style Shop. There, I became more the professional barber under their guidance, one taught me how to cut hairstyles with scissors, this lady gave me my first Oster 76 clippers and taught me how to apply them properly and precisely, and from their my gift did the rest. The other woman insist I pay bills on time or before time, and the other taught me about the civil right movement. And how the black churches was afraid to have Dr. King attend their churches because of the bombs and arsonist threats. These women were groundbreaking entrepreneurs in our neighborhood, not many women cut hair back when I were young in the early seventies and eighties; and they were great barbers and great hairstylist, they had a large clientele to teach me from, they competed with another great barber shop in our community, the Carter's Brothers, I tried to work there first, but it was *a family business* only. And they inspired us to get our own business as well. To get a haircut in their shop, you had to get up early to get a number between a hundred to be in line, and you saved up ten dollars just to go there for a cut; which equivalent to today's market cost of twenty-five dollars. I also worked at the most renown shop in Birmingham; The Etheridge Brothers Barber Shop, under a great mentor Mr. John Etheridge. He was a wise man, I learned from him a lot about business, and how to razor shave professionally; he made great business decisions, and process education differently than anyone I have met to date. He didn't graduate from schools, but became a very successful businessman, became a Millionaire with his relentless attitude, and faith. *He always said, "Somebody Need Some Sense"... "And Money Is Calling Your Name"... "And They Will Get Up When They Stomach Call They Name; They Not Hungry Enough Yet"...* this was my early introduction to how black business professional helped the youth. Thirdly I discovered my athletic talents, and so did other schools, and they came recruiting my services in the eighth grade, could've gone to a private school named Holy Family High

School; but my mother insisted I go to school of her choice, but by now I am feeling unfulfilled, and frustrated with my current life. All the things I felt I could have experienced and encounter with my gifts, and where they could've taken me, far away from my current conditions. I thought opportunities had passed me by, because of decisions I had no consent of my own to make. But at eighteen, I could leave home, and go on my own, at last my change will come, but I was not equipped to handle my decisions properly, confused at this point in what I should do, thought about the military, almost signed up, but end up going to *Dr. A. G. Gaston Business College on fifth avenue, Downtown*, played on the basketball team there, was scouted, then got invited to come to *Miles College, the Golden Bears,* given a full scholarship, felt like finally I can freely choose my own course in life, without parental advisory, felt like the best years of my life, on the dean list, playing a sport I loved, and through much earned *self determination* I arrived, I thought; see after being cut from my high school basketball team two years in a row, after making it to the final cuts both time, they chose the big and tall guys over me in each tryout, from that day onward I was determined to dunk on them as often as I saw them under the goal, and I did with ease, they nicknamed me "Air Jap" because of my gift to play above the rim. Now finally on a startup college team, the first coach loved me, had me starting my freshman year, but the school released him, and a new coach arrived, he loved me too, but in a different way, right before the regions began he didn't want to waste my freshman year playing with these class of players; so he called me into his office, and gave to me at that time in my life the most disappointing advise and news, but looking back, it was the best advice for future rewards... *"Daryl, I Will Have To Redshirt You" this year, go to class, come back next season, and play with my new recruits.* He wanted me to play with his incoming recruiting class. My countenance drop; my spirit were so broken, saying to my young self, my hard work and self determination was tried and tested; and I fail the test, dropped out of school, due to my young self carrying emotional past obstacles forward, so I walked away from a free education, couldn't at that time cope with another stumbling block in my way. Was emotionally drained; but guess what happened in the following year; Miles basketball team won the chip without me. It was a hard pill to swallow; (but another lesson learned about giving up prematurely because something was taken away you work hard to get)...So I went home, back to blocks in which I were raised on, and hustled the wrong way this time due to some bad choices again, I nearly got killed, discovered faith, got out them streets, and off them blocks, started back my entrepreneurial goals and saved the necessary money using my gifts, back working at Etheridge Brothers again, and two years there afforded me the opportunity to open my own shop after many early morning and late nights cutting hairstyles. (sidebar) Salute to "the brickyard" who helped me be self determined, they push me to improve each day my skills to win, and to be the best of the best. Therefore I named my first business in homage of our competitive nature, "The Best Of The Best Barber And Style Shop" of course. It was the community favorite shop in Ensley at that time, I was twenty-five years of age when it was established, it were a runaway success; turned things around in my life and inspired many of my peers to do the same, wouldn't had it no other way. See mentoring and counseling young black men for greatness is definitely necessary and needed now. That's why Thank everyone and everything that inspired my mental state of wealth. For every mile of my life is the inspiration behind this how to book; it's not about glorifying money as power, it's not about glorifying the power of wealthy people; but this book is about the power of information, that's the money game, that's the art of Americanism. Salutations to the Supreme Being for all lessons, and many more to come that I want fail; nor quit on, but with resolution, keep creating informative solutions. Love you all. Asè.

Daryl D. Jones, Sr.

Chapter 1

First: How to be free from mental poverty? *"there must be a definite of purpose with a burning desire to make a difference in our families and in the world"*...So what makes Americanism the finest system in the information age, in the world; especially when compared to others, it's simple. There are six pillars that established this Country's wealth and prosperity over many nations in such a short period of time in human history. A collective idea called, *'We the people', 'by the people';* today Americans are enjoying many incentives other nations are still in need of; but many times this Country's stability and credibility were on the verge of collapsing due to the deficits collected from borrowing goods and services, companies outsourcing jobs and the lack of jobs for laborers here. Our creditworthy ratings was in question by the loaning Nations that supported us not too long ago. But the **stability** of Americanism and the fight for sovereign independence caused 1. we the **free government** (*rights and freedoms afforded by we the people);* networking with 2. we the **free** and **self determine industrial entrepreneurs** (*titans of commerce)*; networking with 3. we the **free banking system** (we the *security exchangers and depositors* of *currencies*); networking with 4. we the **free insurance market system** (*the people's burial, healthcare, merchant insurances)*; while networking with five and six; we the **free** and **sovereign** people attempting to constituted a declaration of 5. **Liberty and** 6. **Justice** *(for all it's free citizens), these six pillars of stabilization,* *and defiant attitudes regardless of the founding members racial intentions in drafting the original constitution.* See no matter the intention or personal interest of the found members these six implemented pillars of Americanism kept no one in Americanism from the pursuit of freedom, no one should fail at the pursuit of happiness either (the ownership of property) with self determination. So is it "**Mental**" or **Misinformed students**? Let's travel the matrix of the "**Mental Poverty**", but let's start by suggesting the **Mental** aspect first in the adjective diction, the word is relating to the (**Mind**), or our mental faculties. This word is synonymous with "**intellectual property rights**" which refers to creations of the mind; such as inventions, literatures, artistic works, designs, symbols, names, ISBNs, images, which are used in **commerce**"... The **mental** aspect of the mind can go by many synonyms (*intellectual, cerebral, brain, rational, cognitive*) to detail a few. This word also relating to the disorders of the (**Mind**), synonymous with (*psychology, psychological, psychogenic, psyche, psycho*). The origin is Latin, *(mens, ment, mentails) to* around the late middle English. It was also said in modern time; '*a mind is a terrible thing to waste',* but in all honesty, "***the heart*"** *not the muscle,* but the deepest memory of the mind was weighed on the scale of truth against a feather in the ancient time; it was known to hold the most memories of our accounts. But this "**Mental**" which is the lower self "***the psyche*"** in the **Ka Ab Ba,** known as the tree of life… teaches we must connect with the transcend minds as well. There are passages that say, *"we must love the Supreme Being with all our heart, soul, and mind, and our neighbor as ourselves"; and another one say, "so as a man thinks in his heart, so is he"; and another say, "out of heart flows the issues of life, and the mouth will utter such deeds"; see we have the mental capacity to create our own success or create our own demise within "the Mental" arena of life, we choose our mental destinations.* Now, let's examine **"Poverty"** *the matrix* denotatively describe a state of poor existence. This word got it origin in France, according to the french diction. The Matrix is a noun, that indicates a person can be in such state, a place can be ravaged with such conditions, a thing like soil can yield nearly nothing due to depleted hydrogen and carbon. Last but not the least, "an idea", or teachings or thoughts within our mental environment can restrict wealth and health from manifesting. The etymological word "Poverty" comes from the old French word (*povertè*) or modern French: (pauvreté*)*, from Latin *(paupertās)* from middle English *(pauper, poor)* spoken around the late 12th century, descriptive of the middle ages when peasants, laborers, farmers were given the lowest classes or social status in society. Many were entitled to minimum returns, though they labor relentless to become free tenants. Was restricted from land ownership, or titleholders under feudalism; that's when the small lords of the royal order took control of local lands in many areas where they attached slaves to the land through (serfdom) to work claimed lands. **Poverty** was a designated system implemented by the lords *of* France to gain agricultural wealth from the peasants or slaves of that time. We know the history of such confiscation of land till this very day. So now what is the true path to freedom or the way of escape from mental poverty. **It is land ownership, or land control.** To become **landlords,** to be **titleholders** of land free and clear. For the power and knowledge that the higher classes in the social, economic, and political status have are knowing the importance of land. The history of wars are over land confiscations, and extraction of resources. Land would be our inheritance, if were not for displacement and the economic gain of chattel property. See the need for slave labor, and establishing sovereignty, are to have lordship over land. It is business and profitable. Our Illustrious Crown, our real status or respected status or the lordship rights of land, are our wealth and freedom. We cannot be free from mental poverty, displaced from land and not redressed (set right or remedy). For what the land warriors did against the original occupants of the land was sanctioned feudalism. It was business under contract laws (called treaties) not constitutional yet. Everyone need a mass of land to call home, ask the black indigenous people who once lived carefree and settled happily with nature on their land before their challengers arrived. We know and heard the stories, but never were told or taught the the truth or the dirty secrets about land and resources, first starting with the control of the Mother Continent of Africa, and America; *but here some helpful tips: we can find properties or land* *to buy at your local county court house through tax deed or tax lien auctions; but set up a trust with the county clerk or a private trust that can protect our land and property we purchase. We must purchase land through a common law trust, under a Real Estate Investments Trust Companies (R.E.I.T) get with a professional trust attorney and begin to establish generational wealth, by correcting our uniform commercial code as well our (UCC-1); this form corrects our financial statements as secured party creditors, then register the documents in probate with the Secretary of the State's office.* Get an expert to help us follow the instructions properly (**AV Financial**). It's legal to do. Freedom from **Mental poverty** depends on a shift in how we act upon information. Land raiders are real, stop being peasants in our thinking. No more laboring to make others rich only, time to negotiate as merchants, producers and traders; time for **land** equality. Time to work our own land, barter from our own land, sell produce from our own land, build our homes on our own land, that's our profitable sweat equity, have courage to be rich, go forth, as the passage says, *"be of good spirit, be courageous, have no fears, for the Supreme Being is in us and with us; we* deserve real tangible wealth. **Land** is what "**Wealthy People**" do first. It is recorded that the Queen Of England is the largest trust titleholder of land, amassing ⅛ of the world's land (*8,000 million of acreage*). It is also recorded that Ted Turner holds in trust a *million acreage of land*. The confederate south promised over fifteen thousands black soldiers who fought in civil wars, (forty acreage of land and mules to farm it free and clear; to redress them after and during the reconstruction era; a ***promissory note*** was issued before the civil war ended with the north). We know the promissory note was not honored after the wars ended against the Union army. This transferred the ownership of land and wealth by winning the land rights. The "***Emancipation Proclamation***" transition their southern citizens to a united land under the federal government. Remember civilized free people own their land free and clear of statutorily interference before the civil war. We must become again the people who will discover resourceful extractions on **Our Own Land** *" in order to be* prosperous and be rewarded tremendous wealth through land development. This is now our "doctrine of discovery" we can own land. Be a great landlord, work the land, no time for excuses especially in knowing the truth; no more room for mental poverty because of laziness; freedom at last will come when we do for our family first, when we're free on sovereign land. I know there are constant rhetoric on poverty and it adverse effects on the black communities, mostly because of the land displacement for sure. So it's by design many are homeless, better yet landless, because land benefit prudent people, the wisest merchants, or the smartest traders, we know now that **land** equate to wealth. It's not hard to breakthrough **"Mental Poverty"**, and be richly rewarded with land and resources; you can do it alone as an individual but its greater as an investment group, because we must learn how to do commerce and compete for our percentages of the wealth pie as a group. Remember to set up our *Irrevocable Private Trust* to protect our beneficiaries, our land, and our resources; we will need an expert trust to guarantee the sovereign title holding of the estates. Now, remember the facts, **"When In The Black"** we own; better yet control our land, our resources, and our estates free and clear in order to obtain the quality of life we deserve as living organic being, (seek out a **Common Law Trust**). Asè.

Chapter 2.

Second: How to define security? *"there must be a clear plan of action to secure our ideas, thought and imaginations".* Now let's examine the mindset of Americanism and the trillions of dollars spent at the taxpayers expense on defending this great country. The militia alone is one of most advanced in the world, but we still get infiltrated, but safer than most nations. So this word **"Security"** and it's matrix is denotatively describing the word **"Security"** *literally as the quality of being safe, having assurance, a state of safety. Therefore this noun* denotes reliability in withstanding pressure, force, or stress. An act to defend a person, a place, a thing, or an idea. "**Security**" is on the majority of our minds; whether it be socially, economically, or politically. Protection is built around these encompassing obligations to secure Americans interest. The trillions in fiat currency along with created debt instruments like: (homesteads, *municipal bonds, railroad bonds, utility bonds, water and sewer bonds, constructional bonds, and equipment bonds, and many more we can invest in for fixed returns, at the same time helping to build our nation*) these debt equities are generated to protect our infrastructure, and to protect our free market from foreign and domestic invasions (looters). See this country go to immeasurable means to ensure security for cyberspace technology in order to protect its citizens from the domestic and global hackers. Billions of dollars spent annually on Firewalls to combat data and information age hackers, still don't give us a sense of security; equal protection for Blacks been under benign and neglect, these black codes of non ethical practices were put in effect under President Richard Nixon administration and with all these investments in security, we are still breached and compromised as a race group. We in "the new game of war" for information and data control (*major asset class to invest in*); every since Mr. Nixon's end of the gold standard in the seventies. Our consumer and commercial identities are being compromised for lack of digital security. But the original system of auctioning to the highest bidders still exists to steal wealth and worth. The Government, Residential and Commercial businesses spend annually on surveillance, and security systems. But with all the focus on human safety, or lack thereof; we can't rid the black communities of poverty, crime, and brutality with all this so called security. But with "**When In The Black**" money we the black entrepreneurs and politicians can use our influence to secure wealth in our communities in order to compete in the race for wealth, power and respectful status. We must secure group economics, wealth building and constructional development for our lowest income class to truly have global equality. For nothing has changed since the eve of the eighteen-sixties after the wars for the black's civility and placement into the American construct. So with all the wealth distribution staying the same every since the conception of Americanism, even before and after the reconstruction era, so what ways are there to decrease the wealth gap in this socially engineered and politically constructed system? Oh, there's an answer, "**Security**" this solution goes undervalued, and rarely taught to impoverish people, especially the black households; unless we inquire this concept from wealthy mentors, expert investors, over the counter traders or successful entrepreneurs we want be given any education to gain the knowledge to protect our money. See, *hedging* against losses with **assets** and **asset classes** are how we compete in the race for wealth, without this knowledge, we have no real chance for economic equality. **Security** can go by other names in the market. Investors will say,

*"Stocks" or "Shares" or "Certificates" or "Debt
Security" (Bonds). In the simple definition, a (Security) is
an investment instruments that represents either an
ownership interest in or a debt obligation (bonds) of a
company. The investor becomes part owner in a company
by buying shares or stock certificates or securities of
company.* A (**Security**) is traded on the floors of stock
exchanges, like: (*NYSE*) (*CBOE*) (*CME*) and many other
(OTC) the -over-the-counter markets. For the (OTC) is an
inter-dealer market, linking exchange terminals to (NASD)
National Association of Securities Dealers or the Nasdaq.
Traders don't transact business face to face this way as
they do on stock exchange floors. There are two terms to
real security or real wealth accumulation, "***Equity and
Debt Equity, both investment Instruments***"; and both
can be good for short and long term investing. Remember,
"**Securities**" represent equity or ownership in companies.
So with these variable contracts available on the open
(public) and closed (private) markets we can access asset
classes to generate and create accessible liquid wealth
potentially by applying these three easy to follow formulas
to wealth. 1. **Assets**- *what we own, cash depositories,
accounts receivables, (money owed to us, like rental
payments or loan payments), titles, inventory,
investments,etc.* 2. **Liabilities**- *what we owe, withdrawals,
accounts payables (money we owe creditors). These short
term and long term debt and other obligations such as
mortgages, cars, credit cards, student loans, etc.* 3.
Equity- *the excess of the value of "**Assets**" over the value*

of *"**Liabilities**" that is, our* **Net Worth.** *"We are only what we worth"... I'm reminded of a passage which says, "cast our "Net" out into the deep water, and let it down, for a catch, for sure".* Now that we see the differences in what we thought "**Security**" denotatively meant, the connotative suggestions are more lucrative once learned correctly, and can definitely build more affluent communities; for this will secure a better outcome for us and for our estates. Most people want security but going about their daily activities throwing away their money on mediocre things that depreciating, while consistently failing at securing their families. Let's start our legacy from this day forward, to put our family worth in the annals of human history, and to ensure wealth with our children, grandchildren, and future grandchildren; we will need to establish our first generational trust fund with real asset classes, we will need to be fully invested in*: (stocks; bonds; currencies; futures; precious metals or (precious metal refinery accounts or IRAs for gold bars) real estate; royalties, intellectual properties, patents, infrastructures, land, etc.)* And leave in our **(will)** real securities. For real **security** like this will write our name in the book of life ever after. (*Remember this tip: spread out the inheritance to our beneficiaries, to avoid some tax penalties on the trust in three installations; when they're older than forty-five, wiser at fifty-five, and exempted at sixty-five*); Think about all the good things we can have carried out in our last will and testament, by securing our estates. There many great examples already proven this work in the past like Dr. A.G.

Gaston, and many more great men and women, they've done great philanthropic works we benefactors of. So setting up these different kinds of funded trust companies for great causes, will ensure many of our children's future substantially. The Dr. A. G. Gaston Boys Clubs of America, in Birmingham saved many of us from the poor neighborhood conditions, and many kids who play now are because of the charity their parents received from wealthy individuals like Mr. Gaston in time past. We must attest with all honesty that earning a tremendous salary in today's market is because of prudent investors or because of wealthy philanthropic charitable trust funds. Poor thinking people are sustain in my opinion because of these wise men and women visions and grace toward humanity. Their **Charitable Trust funds** rescued countless of kids from poverty, crime, and death, so when we see **"Security"** its more than safety devices, securing areas, and relationship goals, which are important, but not much of a help against being poor. We and our mates can't remain in poverty, and in love, even if we're secured with iron bars on every entrances of our apartments or homes inside gated communities; and the financial struggles continue; we will eventually suffocate the air out of the room with frustration, someone will eventually cause a riff emotionally, and this can pull us apart inevitably; because of our foolishness with money, *(remember wealth don't always equate to love either, but it will ensure plenty admirers to choose one from to grow in love with)*. With Knowledge like this, we and our mates can become the first of our family's history to shift this wealth paradigm, and become the first pairing of our wealth building teams; *remember the first level of the secured mastermind alliance is in plain sight, in front of us.* Now go forth and define our own lifestyles and secure our own Future with real "**Security**" or "**Asset Classes**" remember "**When In The Black**", *we are secured participants in owning and controlling assets in our portfolio of life.* So go wisely select us a licensed financial experts, a trust lawyer and a CPA in order to secure our investments and to protect our prudent choices for our families, communities and charities. Asè.

Chapter 3.
Third: How to conquer the red (liabilities)? *"Let love, passion, and good choices guide us, and stop to celebrate our successes". "For we are more than the conquerors of Greece and Rome, when we unite in the God who loved us".* Now what is this "**Red**" you may be thinking, *"like what's love got to do with it"* just everything. See "**Red**" is defined in many cultures differently, most time as an

adjective describing nouns, but the matrix still apply to a person pigment, a place like Saturn, a thing like colors, an idea like *red lining areas for credit approvals.* As an adjective "**Red**" is of a color at the end of the spectrum next to orange and opposite of violet. Examples: '*look at her red ruby necklace' or "red is the main chakra".* But as a noun "**Red**" *is color or pigment ranging from yellow to deep red, even blood red.* The origin of the word is Latin (*re, red, back, again*). But the etymology is ancient, The Kushite/Kamitic God was called Re or Ra (Amen Ra or Amun Re) as a description of the Sun Energy or Life Source or Life Force. "**Red**" is one of the first color used in prehistoric arts, tribal people painted their faces with such reddish pigment made from (*ochre*) before ceremonies. The Greeks, The Romans celebrated victories in red body paint after their conquest, most flags are red, many red carpet events, symbolic rituals, and so on. I can go on for centuries on the significance of "**Red**" But I am writing about a cautionary "**Red**" in a monetarily aspect; red as a **deficit** or a **debt owed**. Most companies say being in the "**Red**" or *being in a "hole", defines too many liabilities, loss of capital, owing money to creditors, or owing vendors.* Being in the "**Red**" is a problem when it comes to capital valuation. The company is being depleted, and they are spending more money than they are actually bring in, or have in their account in the bank. They are insufficient, when they need to be more efficient and therefore they owe fees and money to the investors, banks, creditors, vendors, etc. That's not how we conquer being in the

"Red". We must pay our debts off, or don't create debt we can't afford in the first place, we losing our ability to grow wealth, we losing profit. The money game, is like the Monopoly board game, in order to become a great player of assets, our accumulation of wealth is needed, so when someone roll the dice, and fall on our land with properties on it we purchased already, they must pay the landlord in order to move forward depleting their purchasing power. Also remember the roll of the dice with our own money can also land us bankrupt or in jail. Prudent people own and control public and private companies through commerce, for it's all business for the wealthy thinkers. Back to the money game; now because we have an **equity** position and became our own **bank** in the money game, now we are not responsible for borrowing money from the bank and can't be held liable for any debt borrowed against the bank, this how we avoid prosecution. So what advantage is there in purchasing good or services we can't pay for in the first place? We destroying our credibility, and putting ourselves in a tough spot to manage our accounts, and lose the ability to gain account receivables. Staying out of the **"Red"** in this sense, is made for the prudent decision makers; for the prudent rule their outcome, by protecting their income. The only **"Red"** sign we should get use to is **"Stop!"** Stop being disrespectful toward our money. I heard a passage say, " *a fool with his money will separate"; and "it is easy to get money from foolish people"; and it's difficult or unlikely that foolish people maintain their grip on acquired wealth*". We get the picture about being in the "**Red**" now. So the way to conquer the "**Red**" is by remaining in the "**Black**", *we must maintain a surplus, grow our bottom line, and collect assets. **Think**! We are businessmen, and family love is law; the first law to keep close to the heart. Now it's clear that we love ourselves by paying ourselves the first tenth; and then the second tenth to a charity of our choice (human rights, churches, schools, hospitals, shelters, etc.) and Third, take forty percent to invest in **assets and asset classes.** Become investors, merchants, entrepreneurs, silent or principal partners, inventors, traders, etc. And the last forty percent invest in education, insurances (**tip: invest in Viatical Settlements, whole life annuities and term life policies);** living expenses and vacations. It will take discipline and patient, for it's not one way to win races to wealth, it definitely not a sprinting contests either; it's going to take mental endurance to accumulate lasting wealth.* So mastermind our investment plans, and for now on, *"**When In The Black**"*, our resourceful thinking will not let us lack any good money visions we have to help our families, communities, and charities . *"**And together we have visions**... Asè.*

Chapter 4.

Fourth: How to locate directions in the marketplace?

"We can win at being our creative selves knowing that the right time is now, to trust our visions"... Having vision will *"be the light of our path and a lamp to our feet"... "See the only power is green power, so if there's a demand, supply it".* This is the power of the American psyche, learning how this verb **"locate"** is utilized; locate explaining we must place, or set in a particular spot, or position accurately our black market. This middle English word **"locate"** come from a Latin diction *(locātus, past) (loco, to place)* or *(locus, place)*. See many assets have to be purchased, claimed or warranted by locating the place. They will not be placed in our laps, we must learn market terminologies when it come to asset classes; and we must learn OTC traders terms, like: **"locate direction"** and **"Set"**. See in market trading we S.E.T. the (S)Top for losses; our (E)ntry for timing; and our (T)arget for gains. We live on the automated systems and our opportunity for money is right in front of us. It's in the palm of our hands, such as our tablets, cell phones, and computers. The chance for gains is within split seconds, but will we pull the trigger on potential profits. The market **"Direction"** is good no matter what the asset classes are that being traded; remember to be detached from loses are not possible, losing at something is inevitable, but if we be discipline, patient, and manage our forty percent risk capital (*remember if we don't we eventually want have any risk to manage at all if we foolish*). Now let's understand **"Direction"** and the

matrix of this word. Listen, this noun cover many spectrums, its origin is Latin *(dīrēctiō, stern) from the late middle French (direccioun) to the late thirteenth century English.* But **arranging in line**, or **straightening** describe this word best. *"See our true remedy to wealth is not to be seen, but to be led in the right direction; or "if we stay on course long enough and sternly invested in every direction eventually we'll be the heads and not the tails of our lives".* When we have a common direction and taught not to fear market indicators. We can execute and attack opportunities offered in the market. See in order to **"locate direction"** we must straighten out our fears of something we're not privy to learn. Learning about money can be frightening to black folks, it's a lot like a foreign languages, unless we take a secondary language in school to release the veil on our minds; it's all confusing, the same with money solutions, most blacks need to see it first, before they do it first, because of all the broken promises and misuse of our friendship as a people. We need to know losing are experiences of how to win over time, there's no wrong way in the market, it's just business strategies, and many takes it emotionally or personally, it's just the wrong strategy. Here are some directions not explained to our communities. Store to memory, the symbolisms of Wall Street in the use of **"bull"** and **"bear"** to describe the trading market; comes from how these animals attack their opponents. A **bull** thrusts it's horns up into, while a **bear** swipes it's paws downward into. These animalistic actions are metaphors for directional movement in **"Asset**

Classes" in the market. Whereas a strike *up* or *long* is "**bullish**" and a strike *down* or *short* is "**bearish**" A **bullish** market is when the **demand** is up on goods and services, the stock orders are being filled, therefore the price of the share will rise; and a **bearish** market is when the **supply** orders are there, but the **demand** for them are *down*, so the stock price of the goods and services drops. A market can be identified as a gathering of specific or specialized items were people are defending their space to trade the best in the psyche of Americanism or Capitalism. For many markets have existed for as long as people have engaged in trade. One of the richest men in ancient time that was known for his trading genius was Mansa Musa. It was recorded that he gave out gold to people, as he passed through the markets. There are different ways to **locate direction**. In the modern days we identify markets with race groups or ethnicities. They are directing certain market capital or cartels from the global wealth pie to their race group for example: Jews: Diamonds, Banking, Entertainment, Politics; Arabs: Oil, Tourism, Human Trade; Italians: Organized Syndicates, Fashion, Textiles, Shoes; Columbians: Coffee, Narcotics; Asian: Beauty Products, Nails, Automotive, Technology; India: Outsourcing, Hair Extension, Gas Stations; Cubans: Cigars; Irish: Beers; French: Wineries, and so on. We must develop a specialized niche for the specialize buyers or consumers as well. A sovereign black cartel and recognize how direction in the market systems are located in race groups. There two broad classes of market, namely retail or wholesale. There's three time periods in the markets, a very short period, short period, and a long period market. Markets have 3 trading areas, (local, national, international). The definition of a **"Market"** is- *one of many varieties of systems, Institutions, procedures, and infrastructures, whereby traders engage in exchange. Most people exchange by using the bartering systems, the laboring systems or the purchasing systems, this how prices for goods and services are established and produced* . But I am here to share something the majority of the people do not consider. Too often goes ignored, in order to generate liquid wealth. The stock exchange, or the mercantile exchange where majority of people is only taught one asset class (*common stocks*) the less lucrative and most volatility of all the asset classes. There's other lucrative asset classes to learn how to invest in for profitable returns relating to trade or commerce (commercial interest); yes every investment has risk involved, but we can wisely leverage these **options and variable contracts**. (*See, the black community need a shift of wealth to the mercantile classes*). Do we want larger profit potential, less risk, high probability on our returns, well learn and invest in intangible and tangible asset classes and mercantile classes like: *Futures; Foreign Currencies (Forex); Options; ETFs; Gold; Precious Metal; (now Crypto-Currencies*, and Block-chain Technology) Start purchasing tangible and intangible asset classes and mercantile classes. Trained traders open accounts through discount exchanges or direct trading stations, and by acquiring federal trade licenses to import and export mercantile classes over sea. We just need to learn how to locate directions, for we can make money either way, (bullish or bearish) (up or down) we can make money if we're trained properly, we can earn an annual percentage rate that will grow over the long haul for generations. Remember you or a group can open a direct brokerage account with trade exchanges or become a direct trader locally, nationally, and Internationally. Get with a group, or let a veteran investor train us their techniques, or go to a trade academy. There several trader's platforms out there like tradestation.com and many other. Be ProActive Investors, be self determine to manage our resources, our money, our collective power by taking forty percent of our income and self direct our money, diversified our portfolio, don't rely solely on our employer's 401(k) or 501(k) saving accounts or our retirement plans like: 503(b); SEP (Simplified Employee Pension); Keogh plan and etc. For with these managed fund plans we're paying ballooned fees over the years for leaving it in the hands of our brokers to manage, but investment brokers or wealth managers are needed in our **Mastermind** teams; they are good at investment strategies, always seek an expert financial advisers for our brokerage needs, (*Tip: ask our brokers to wave our 12b-1 fees upfront, in order to save on fees early in the investment planning*); but educating and training ourselves as financial representatives, brokers, and managers would be best for our race to win the race to wealth. (security examines are arranged in series, from series 6 to 63 seek details). But for now we can take control of our retirement plans and invest the money wisely in "**Gold**", **or** "**Gold IRAs**" and other **"asset classes"** through these two tax deferred saving accounts. (Traditional IRA and The Roth IRA) they are great rollover vehicles from our 401(k) or 501(k) savings to compound our investments for long term growth (see if you qualify income wise) they have tremendous tax deferred advantages, but the tax deductions different in both and tax fees on withdrawals are different in both. Remember these are part of multiple streams of income once we're at a fixed income age like seventy years old. (Sixty-two and half exempt us from local property taxes and lower our tax rates on earned income); but if we are employed don't retire early it will affect our earning potential from our social security benefits by accepting payouts at fifty-nine and half in a lower income bracket, first raise our income bracket, for the more money we earn, and place in social **security** the more the payouts; but with patient, discipline and being proactive professional investors operating "*in the wealth zone*" as self directing traders, we want have to fear minimum loses, stay within the rules, place a entry, establish a target, and set a stop, no matter what we invest in, and leave the house, and enjoy our lives. We know investing all we have is dumb, invest only what we willing and able to lose, don't gamble our money away taking chances on becoming rich overnight, the stock market or any market can and will eat us alive being pigs greedy for the money, why get trapped chasing carrots like rabbits, looking for the dangling money without power, there's a passage which says," *for if we are faithful in the little, we will be faithful with much"; "and don't despise small beginnings, not many days from now, we will rejoice, in our abundance"*. We can steer our own wealth plan annually, establish an asset allocation fund system that suit us, and when we do what I recommend in this how to book, and distribute our money prudently, take one day at a time gathering up **asset classes** and locate the right directional timing in the market, by remembering to be patient, discipline, and non emotional about loses, and take a little time to celebrate our successes, prudently. The market will eventually benefit the buyers, and the sellers, so seize the opportunity when one appear, when we know that we can take the risk and manage the risk within the budget, go for it. Just establish our core strategies to compete and attempt to win, by never forgetting to seize the opportunities in plain sight, right in our face. So discipline, patient with the market strategies; and the applied sciences of wealth and power. We don't never have to gamble all our money, unless we take a portion of it to risk on potential profits, that the wealth strategies of "**When In The Black**". Asè.

Chapter 5.

Fifth: How to see opportunities in front of us? *"The only opportunity to make a difference is now, tomorrow not promising chances"*....It is said, *"in the middle of difficulty lies opportunity"*. It is also said, *"a pessimist sees the problems in every opportunity, an optimist sees the opportunity in solving every problem. We must be our own change, for opportunities favors the bold"; "and to ensure opportunity doesn't pass, recognize it in plain sight."* The matrix of this word **"Opportunity"** is a noun. The origin is Latin (*opportunus, opportunitas*); old French (*opportunite*); old English (*opportune*); late middle English (*opportunity*). *This plural noun is define as a set of circumstances that makes it possible to do something, to chance, an occasion, a moment, a opening, a option.* Noticing opportunities will give us the possibility to improve communities; remodel apartment complexes, build holistic hospitals, purchase land for farming, and sub divisions, and so on... The questions are, can we recognize the opportunity at building sustainable commerce? Can we organize investment groups? Can we connect culturally, emotionally, economically as black people? Once these answers are emphatically yes, we will need vision, for sustainable wealth is made possible when we secure opportunities in front of us, for examples, whenever we're seeking life changing events, or career opportunities, or wealth building projects; we must pursue degrees or acquire specialized skills we do not have in our communities to help build a functional black commerce district with proper protection in place. See to collectively build a better neighborhood for our families, communities, and humanity we have to embrace opportunities before gentrification does. Many mastermind teams become allies to hedge their opportunities for resources and returns on investments. So what's important about seeing opportunities? Are they invisible to lazy people? Are they all around us in our urban areas? Yes, That's why I'm writing this how to book, to help us be alert, and creative, and see in plain sight, a simple platform, called community or commerce development. This concepts is the oldest asset plan we have in the world, to meeting our expectations, and changing our current conditions. Learning how to develop a specialized skill and trading systems with a particular good or service, will place us and our skills into the competitive market. Therefore we'll have to compete with our market competitors when going in business, or developing commercial districts, or building subdivisions. So our focus when possible should be on high tier production with a high price point, we will need less sales to make higher potential returns. But first, we become retailers, wholesalers, distributors, merchants, manufacturers, traders, etc. Remember any low priced production for sale is wiser and better than wages on a job. Products or services are sometimes requested at customer's demand, this is good only when we can supply such demands, this kind of special services will determine our **Net** or **profits** as well. But there are other opportunities if we only knew where to find them.

Remember we have to be taught the simple terminologies and strategies to apply. 1. **Liquid Assets**, this opportunity is right in front of us (*our currency, cash, money, dollars*) which requires less spending and more investing than traditionally working hard; it only require prudent applications. Learn the counterparts between liquid and non liquid. "A *liquid asset is mostly currency (cash) on hand or an asset class that can be readily converted to money. Liquid assets are investments readily converted into cash once realised or cashed. a more lucrative liquid asset class to invest in is needed inventory: (examples: alkaline water systems, and organic agriculture) This will be a great healthcare plan for our communities.* I recall a passage which says, "*wisdom is "the principal thing"(the original amount something cost before interest applied or the highest ranking position); and with all our getting, get understanding"*... It vitally important to get understanding of financial liquidity. **Financial liquidity** can settle current **liabilities** either for our companies or individually. Acquiring **liquid assets** can relieve stress related systems on the cost of living, and when these assets are sold or realised or cashed in, they are barely affected with fees, most times it has accrued interest that compounding over years especially when placed in the correct investments plans. (examples: *equities, royalties, interest bearing accounts, saving bonds, certificate of deposits, insurance policies (tip: invest in viatical settlements); commercial papers, promissory notes, bearer bonds, Treasury bonds, Treasury bills, Treasury notes, Ginnie*

Mae certificates, and many more); many of these has maturity rates and dates with interest already accrued to them, worthy of purchasing for short or long term turnarounds. Most are readily accessible and retain value, very seldom an **asset** lose valuation. (*examples are: stocks; bonds; futures, foreign currencies (Forex); crypto-currency; titles; (examples: copyrights, trademarks, patents, royalties, land; cars; houses; unclaimed Inheritances, wills*); *municipalities (stocks and bonds) or corporate debt equities (bonds); precious metals; gold; silver; ETFs; inventory; equipment, rentals; manufacturing; distribution; retail; wholesale; warehouses, and e-commerce;* there many more, unlike most **Non- Liquids** assets, these potential assets are real estate investments, because this could take months or years to receive cash or currency easily and readily from the sales. Real Estate has tremendous advantages and disadvantages, let's examine closely this *non liquid liability or asset; (as a mortgage payment it is a long term debt; we are responsible for all repairs, can be trapped for years when banks dangling equity lines of credit in our faces, unless we have a definite plan of action for borrowing against the equitable position in our house, we can go into default, and face foreclosure on the origination; and will affect our FICO consumer credit score for years. Two: we will never own or control our titles, deeds, or warrants free and clear to put in our trust as long as we are liable for such debt), do not get trapped in fancy arms rates* *(adjustable rate mortgages) or long term fixed rates either. Three, if we purchase such debt put fifty percent down with a fixed rate at five to ten year terms; this how we invest or control our equity going in, see with fifty percent down, we can do interest only terms as well, (ask for the libor rates if possible) we still can pay on the origination separately, but don't get relaxed with the low monthly interest payments, we still have the principal or origination payments owed, so pay both, but send more toward the principal or origination regardless of the terms we choose. Of course a house can be an asset by wholesaling, developing, rehabbing, or generating rental payments; (but even that depend on buyers or occupancy); another way is through lease option agreements (if you want to flip the house over time); and there are few other ways to benefit from real property investing: (tax lien, tax deeds, tax lien funds). Network with a expert licensed realtors in order to bid on foreclosure sites like: Hud.gov or hudhomestore.com or GinnieMae.gov or bankforeclosureslisting.com or MLS listings to gain these non liquid but profitable investments. (we will need our company or our individual bank cashier's check to complete the transactions at the closing); try bank owned short sales too, lawyer's inventory, and many other options. I recommend we set up an LLC. A limited liability company or a (Real Estate Investment Trust Company);* this a great strategy for long term

diversification, all real estate can help fund our trust company; we need to purchase real estate for our beneficiaries and remember we should have a trust lawyer to write our grantor wishes (the creator of the trust) and carefully pick noble qualified board members who can carry out our desires. Most entities that holding real estate are setup as a irrevocable private trust or a charitable private trust, or a common law trust; this is done to protect and control our free and clear titles, deeds, and warrants. Real Property Statuses are equitable asset classes, but set up a trust for our beneficiaries to benefit generation after generation perpetually. Remember no negative assets value (NAV) are accepted in a trust. Only (CAV) cumulative asset values are; we will acquire investments that accumulate interest or maintain it valuation over the long haul. There two recognizable terms you've heard me say; short term and long term investments strategies throughout this how to book. Our **liquidity** depends on the **asset classes** we purchase, but remember taxation apply if we don't use a tax deferred strategy, or not for profit statuses, and we must consider inflation and the price gap over time on goods and services. We will need plenty of **assets** for future purchasing power. For historically wages doesn't improve or increase to combat the cost of living, so whenever we buy worthless good and services, we can't get appreciation on them in the future. So we will have to invested into appreciated liquidity for the high demand on future goods and services to be affordable, which mean things are going up, but our money don't match or exceeds the demand. The only hope in the future for poor thinkers will be if in demand supplies don't sale, then prices come down. Remember minimum wages to maximum wages are not designed to liberate us on any level collectively, but regardless of the price gap, when our **assets** are **liquid**, our assets can solve many living expenses we'll be liable for in the future, remember this passage, *"a party is thrown for laughter and fun; and wine will hype us up; but money or what's in the highest demand, answer all things".* Now we know flexible opportunities to change our fortunes by having multiple streams of income. Money can compound over time in our equitable instruments, or debt eliminators. But the decisions we make today, will shape our future wealth, worth, and power. Remind ourselves **"When In The Black"**... We learn to see opportunities as investors, merchants, traders, and businessmen. I leave us with this quote I've embraced; *"**our money no good unless it contributes something to our family, community, and charity of choice, unless money builds a bridge to a better life, any person can make money, but it takes a special kind of people to use money responsibly, When In The Black",* Asè.**

Chapter 6.

Sixth: How to secure our Mastermind alliance? *"we are only strong as the links in our chain; for a threefold cord is not easily broken; for two heads are much wiser than one"; "wise decisions are made among wise counsel"...* So securing our **Mastermind** team is necessary before taking action, for it far easier to find help first, than to think we can carry a heavy burden alone. So when going into battle or into negotiations be equipped, for we go in as a team, so no person can prevail against us alone; "**Secure**" is the first matrix we will explore. This adjective connotatively describing a *fixed, fastened, not to give way, or become loose, or be lost kind of message; so let me ask this question: if there was something we care truly for, will we fight for it in order to secure it's safety?* Of course, so this word "**Secure**" is a verb, to take action, like, *"we built and fortified that portfolio wisely, now it cannot be questioned"*... The origin of this word is Latin (*se- cura or without care*) (*securus*) *feeling no apprehension*, spoken mostly in mid 16th century. Secondly, "**Mastermind**" this word matrix is a verb as well (used with object) *meaning to plan and direct (a complex project or activity), skillfully.* Thirdly, "**Alliance**" this word matrix is a noun, the origin is late 12th century middle English; an old French word (*ali(er)*; *to ally*) **Now we know how to master our mental plans securely with an ally**, in doing this we will be able to execute and secure a particular idea, project, or plan. Assembling this key team first will successfully accomplish our task; and again we must ally with two or more expert advisors who are successful in their chosen fields. We will need experts at business startups; business websites; business credit; business funding; business investments; business accounting/taxation; business laws; business banking, business acquisitions, etc. We will need to team up with our families if possible first; '*for how can two walk together unless they agree*"; "*for love starts at home first, then spreads abroad*"; "**family is business, and love is law**"... For most startup investors are in front of us in plain sight. A family member, a close acquaintance, a childhood friend, a co worker, etc. We go to other's means when all else fail, like: (hard lenders, venture capitalists, commercial bankers, loan sharks, etc.) See after we've exhausted our collective options we go to them; in most cases we will need two or more professional business plans, laying out the specifics alongside good credit, and some collateral as security for the loan approval. Remember "**Alliance**" is a noun. Which define a person, a place, a thing, or an idea, done together. Remember I said our partners or alliances are vitally important to our success; the next thing our market selections and locations are very important to our successes; next our niche, our supplies (become suppliers) or services are very important to our successes, and our professional approaches to the market are very important to our successes. A business plan or idea or format is very important to our successes when seeking capital for expansions and acquisitions, and we will need to assemble our **Allies** with these kind of **Mastermind**

abilities, we must continue our business relationships with them, be faithful to growing their bottom line as well; start joint venture agreements, or request referral payments to do business with us, or seek sponsorship contracts with our allies. This how we establish discount rates on services with each other, in order to achieve these market shares. We must always remember these passages.."*we have not because we ask not"; "don't ask doubting results, for that people will receive nothing of me"; "share our idea with experts; our vision with accomplish people, they may run with our plan when they read it"; "and Seek, knock, and ask, and doors shall be open to us"*... We must put together a successful **"Secure Mastermind Alliance"** that bring us, our family, and our communities into financial stabilization and value, if we to grow out of these meager living conditions and lack of professional black commerce, we must demand equality for our purchasing power of one point one trillion dollars. But it starts with the top black income earners working in our communities and the trickle downward effect will ensure employment for us all, but we can't wait for that to happen after all these years of do nothingness. We must establish our **Mastermind** network that extend and expand our vision for change over the long haul, for when we as a people are in demand for more than entertaining other races, and respected because of our great exploits in commerce, then we will be acknowledged in the kingdom of men. See, the **Mastermind** concept has been implemented for ages, it has worked for secret societies; political parties; industrial titans; like **the founders at Vista Equity Partners; Ariel Investments group and AV Financial.** *Several* minority own organizations of all types used this concept and when applied correctly with faith can work for anyone; the question is, do we have an entrepreneurial spirit and a legitimate investment plan? Are we trusting our unwavering fortitude to build our families, our businesses, and our communities? Do we know key people in our lives and in the market with the expertise who can guide or mentor us to the next level of execution? Of course we do, they are in plain sight, they are waiting on us, they were once in our shoes, they had dreams, visions, ideals, and with relentless courage went after them. Stop fearing the unknown, get out of our heads due to past obstacles, and overcome our emotional losses, we not alone, don't quit on ourselves. This how to book is here to encourage our dreams, visions, ideas and our definitive purposes. Now is the time to build great concepts, we deserve more than mediocre communities, or a meagerly existence; there are levels, stages, processes, phases to accomplishing successful plans of action; being successful investors or establishing legacies are not for cookie cutting thinkers. These successes take time and information in order to secure our black heritages, or reach our divine potential in this life, not waiting for the by and by, but now! Get together by bridging our success teams, select noble advisers to help us steer the helm, and find principal partners or alliances and work the plans patiently with those professionals, it will save us money in the long haul;

invest in doing it right the first time. For we know the quote, **"we get what we pay for"**... *"I say avoid the get rich quick talk, for if it look and sound too good to be true, it's probably is"*. Go with the experts we will need for our particular visions. "Prudence *will accommodate prosperity to stick around, because prosperity lives among the prepared"*. Keep reading this book to help pursue the realization of our heart desires, for one of the key factor is choosing to trust ourselves as black people again, for we are enough. Enough greatness in us to convince others by the very works we do; for prudent people seek experts who networking with other experts in their respected fields of expertise. Everyone that makes real millions, billions, or trillions are networking with their alliances. For the expert allies we connect with *must see the end of our vision, at the beginning"*... **So, "When In The Black"**, our hard earned dollars must count by examining who we spend with the most, remember how we handle small relationships with money will determine how we master larger relationships with money. Be honorable in our approach to partnerships or alliances while our visions or companies are small in order to help build up our black communities, and with strategic patient and discipline, we'll be putting together *secure mastermind alliances* that keeps us out of the "**red**" and on path to being in the "**black**" by establishing wealth stabilization programs through arranging sustainable powerful alliances. Asè.

Chapter 7.

Seventh: How to learn from successful mentors? *"The richest man in world started with making mistakes with money; and until he sat at the feet of a wealthy mentor, did he begin to thrive in his mind"... It is said, "our net worth depends on our network"; "our company we keep, determine the company we keep"..."the young in business knows the risk, but the veteran in business knows the exceptions"..."the most important lesson for a young man is to establish credibility, a reputation, and character with another man possessions"... "a young man without ambitions is an old man waiting to die"... "the way for a young aspiring person to rise is to improve his respect in every way, expecting to learn, and not to be hinder by anybody"...* Now, let's "Learn"... This word "**Learn**" it is vital to growth and development; the descriptive matrix is a verb, *which if someone take action to acquire wisdom, understanding, and knowledge of something. So when people can learn a specialized skill through observations, studying, teachings, information, discovering, experiencing, researching*, which are the truest form of education, when these tools are implemented without bias agendas and personal interest many will thrive in our communities. The origin of this word "**learn**" is West Germanic to old English (*leornian*) German (*lernen*); English (*lore*); the old English *(leornian 'learn')* was *connotatively also used in middle English as 'teach'*... *this is why mentorship or mentoring programs* are vitally important to the successes of many at risk youths in our communities. Getting advice or training especially while young can make an impact on the future of our National GDP and Security, and the employment rate will drop drastically. Mentoring will be impactful on our infrastructure; and innovation will increase substantially; when older mentors are involved in the young and great knowledge is passed down, specialized skills are transferable equity to the next generations, and this can change the outcome of what would be tragic stories in our neighborhoods. See without the remedy of mentoring our youth's minds or being advised ourselves, no wealth can last. Now back to this word, "**Mentor**" the matrix of threefold, a noun, plural noun and verb; which describes an experienced and trusted adviser; a trainer; a teacher; a consultant, a tutor; a counselor; a guru. These personal "Mentors" guide scientists, innovators, students, disciples, employees, athletes, musicians, entrepreneurs, etc... The origin of the word is Greek (Mentōr) Latin and French (mentor) spoken mid 18th century via French and Latin but from Greek, it was the name given to the adviser of young Telemachus in Homer's Odyssey. So the learned was the mentor; which in the ancient time, was given to the privileged class. Like today's hidden truths to wealth building are only revealed to those who seek it out or privy to the information. So the best way "**Mentors**" can help prepare future leaders are to expose them to other great achievers, and their secret to successes. Our "**Mentors**" should see more in us, and develop those gifts, and help bring them to forefront. There are helpful books to read or listen to on audio, like: "*Hands Off Manager, How To Mentor People*"; "*The Mentor Leader*"; "*9 Powerful Practices Of Really Great Mentors*"; and "*Philosophy For Successful Living*"... For to name a few that helped me; so whenever we around great achievers pick their brain, be great listeners, let them point us in the right direction; for our talents and abilities alone want make us wealthy, but humility will. We must value learning, for knowledge is priceless, and information is intelligence. If we care about our future and our potential to build wealth, get in the presence of successful "Mentors" who truly cares for us, and will look after our best interest and not just their own. And when the right "Mentors" are in our lives don't waste their years of experience. Their expectation in us is left up to us; make the opportunity worthwhile, by showing them their time, and knowledge is valuable to us. there's a passage I am reminded of, *"if we train confidence in our children in the ways they should go; they will not depart from the instructions; though they may stray; they will return"*. Learn from wise and wealthy **"Mentors"** and soon he will learn from us, and he will gain future wealth from us. People like Mr. Robert Johnson and Michael Jordan position their wealth alliance to purchase the Charlotte Hornets market by constant learning, and now they mentoring and allying with the next innovators, and next great investors, like themselves. Now these up and coming leaders of tomorrow are being groomed as we read this chapter, and this kind of thinking keep them in the Now Money. One of My "Mentors" I've learned from about scheduling our time and planning our visions, is my friend, Richard M. Scrushy, the founder and innovator behind HealthSouth Corporation, he one of the inspirational stories for me to pen this how to book as well, and to know how he persevere in the face of difficult situations and carry on forward with integrity, and to stayed consistent with his faith, and come out on the other side resolved, and ready to solve any problem with supreme confidence. I learned trusting in the plans the Supreme Being have for our lives are through handling hard challenges. See after all his ordeals, he was inspired to write an excellent book... "*When Building A Billion Dollar Company*". He has such a willing heart to help make the world a better place for others even after his own personal setbacks, he silently making a comeback now, he continues to remain passionate in advising the next up and coming fortune 500 companies and new innovators after all he been through. Salute his definitive purpose to help the poor and mentor the next entrepreneurs. So remember to help our young minds early in life, teach them principal things that impacts their lives as they get older especially liquid wealth. Give them books like "**When In The Black**" and have seminars training them how the wealthy keep learning from mentors through book clubs on wealth. See books on wealth can help us write our own narrative, not the story others have written for us; consistently learning is how we become mentors, and that how we see the full potential in others. Go join up with wealth building projects that give us tremendous valuable insight and gain understanding on how competitive markets are builded in communities all over the world. For all the things we desire lies between their ears to ours, and our ears can become doers of wealth and power.. And our worth come when we sit, ask, listen, and then apply; then rinse and repeat, by creating **automatic investors** and **mentors** ourselves with "**When In The Black**" money. Asè.

Chapter 8.

Eight: How to see assets over liabilities? "*We must see ourselves already possessing what is in our heart to have*"; "*this is the victory that has given us the battle, even our faith with works*". "*Now faith (the subconscious mind) is the substance (a particular matter) of things (material things like gold; investments; assets; cash, etc.) hoped for (or expected); faith (the subconscious mind) is the* *evidence (proof or manifested information)* of things *(non material, spirit, intangible) not seen (in our conscious minds)*. Consider the vast evidence of the world or universe. Ask ourselves how we see without the Sun, or how the intricacies of the eyes were designed to need that energy source? Many wonders we had nothing to do with the designing of, consciously; but each one is vitally important to our existence, and our ability to experience the benefits it gives. Our eyes get to see how the sun is responsible for time; food; vegetation; flowers, etc. The same with the brain, and the heart, and the entire body. All these things point to an Intelligent Creator, this Consciousness is Supreme and divinely working in us and through our subconscious mind. Therefore we can see as the infinite intelligence do, but we not seeing the right way, prudently. Let's examine **"See"** the word matrix is a verb; and the word is from middle English, (seen) from old English (sēon) to see, look, behold, vision, perceive, observe, discern, **understand**, **know**. It also from Proto Germanic *(sehwang, to see)* from Proto Indo European *(sek, to notice)*. We must form a mental picture of what we want to gain or achieve by noticing the unseen in our minds. Like being able to **"See"** an "**Asset**"... Accurately we must understand and know the importance of an **Asset**. So when making decisions with our money, we want consume majority of our currency on senseless depreciating liabilities. "**Liabilities**" are canceling our chances to improving our lives. So Let's dive in and be financially educated about them both. So after we execute these Moneybag applications to our lives, we will be richer by following these simple terms in our everyday choices. First, "**Asset**" this word matrix is a noun, which describe, a person should be an asset; a place should be an asset, a thing should be an asset, and an idea should be an asset. An "**Asset**" is a useful or valuable thing, person, or quality idea. The origin is Latin (*ad satis or to enough*) old French (*asez or enough)* Anglo Norman French (*asset or sufficient estate to allow discharge of a will)* asset is also mid 16th century word said as a legal term, expressing a will. In other analogies an "**Asset** is something valuable that a company or person own or control. Often time beneficiaries benefits from the interest generated off the income on assets. **Assets** has book value; market value; residual value; cost value). Cash comes in many currencies (180 plus worldwide) **Assets** *can be inventory, buildings, machinery, equipment, land, promissory note,* *claims, account receivables, copyrights, patents, trademarks, convertible bonds, municipal bonds, preferred stocks, titles, insurance policies (invest in Viatical Settlements) commercial papers, foreign currencies, futures, options contracts, precious metals, gold, silver, platinum, palladium, rhodium, oil, indexes, ETFs, storage rentals, apartments, properties, people, and etc...* Possession of these kind of "**Asset**" classes in holdings will have us gain economic value as an individual, or groups or corporations. When we own or control assets in a private trust or common law trust our "**Asset**" classes will provide future benefits for us and our heritage to receive. These "Assets" can curve future inflation and pay expenses and improve quality of life. There are four corporate categories explaining an "**Asset**" *Current (short term); fixed assets; financial investments assets; and intangible assets (seek details).* Now we can "**See Assets**" and by what kind of purchases we make will determine what kind of money we make and store up for negotiations". Let's release our mental environment from the incarceration of debts or "**Liabilities**", so we can get out of the prison of poor thinking, in order for wealth creation to take place; we must self represent our own mental wealth and hold ourselves liable for borrowing things we can't profit from or afford in the first place, priorities over pleasures. Establish discretionary spending habits that will enable us to avoid senseless "**Liabilities**". Now let's go deeper, to the root of the problems about money... The **miseducation causes fears**, and the **miseducation is systemically** organized that way. Here's what a "**Liabilities**" is. Understand the matrix is a plural noun which mean *"the state of being responsible for something, especially by law. A things for which someone is held accountable, especially a debt or financial obligation.* "**Liabilities**" was first recorded in the late 17th Century, middle English but derived from a Latin word (*ligare or liable*) or French word (*lier, to bind legally*). *"So the people not in their right financial minds want to be held liable of a debt owed and can face legal prosecution by not honoring an obligation"... Looks like liabilities are entrapments to potentially prosecute us for putting ourselves in debt. Being Fools mean slave labor and ruled people. It's just profitable commerce, to keep the permanent consumer class or the permanent underclass. Guess who that is?* I'm reminded of a passage which says, *"just as the rich rule the poor, so the borrower is a slave to* *the lender".* In today's mindsets people are purchasing their own demise with bad debts; people now living in trapped circumstances by begging, stealing, and borrowing bad debts, people gone wild on credit and debit societies (black people) acquiring things of no real value, misusing consumer credit, trading in the opportunity for real wealth for cheap thrills and jail cells. Going for broke has become as American as apple pie. What happened to us wanting real homeownership; not mortgage payments fixed at thirty years of (liabilities or debts). When other groups in Americanism only wanted five or ten year terms, placing fifty percent down or either purchasing a property outright as an investment. And since the nineteen twenties (other race groups in Americanism used "interest only" terms to separate the principal or the origination from the applied gains or the interest on the home loan, to quickly pay off the original debts or principals at the same monthly rate, (why refi mortgages when we can own it and sale it) any mortgage loaners will get their applied gains or interest applied on the loans, that's what we do as loaners and not borrowers; (become mortgage bankers and brokers) But instead we out here buying thirty thousand to hundred thousand dollars automobiles with no equity position to leverage and capitalize from, but involved in the purchases or buying car notes, promise to pay payments, (liabilities, bad debts), instead become (licensed manufacturers, wholesalers, brokers and retail dealerships ourselves importing and exporting automotive inventory with the port authority. Buying and consuming bad depreciating debts just for fake unfulfilled status. Remember the saying, keeping up with the "Joneses" or keeping up with real bad addictions or hooked on it, like mental poverty; for (the free State of Jones) is in Jones County, Mississippi, and if we are being like that Jones County in history, we just transferring land and slave labor over to the new owners, (federal land and federal government). Every since the eighteen sixties wars for wealth control nothing has changed, just under new management. And as it were then, it's recorded now that 63% of "Americans" are one paycheck away from financial catastrophe, and don't have any emergency funds, savings, or investments. But those percentages increased for blacks in the same Americanism, they in debt to the heavens, praying for a breakthrough, but "**liabilities**" or "**debts**" are the cause of the plunging family structure in black homes more so than any other race group. "Many need to use their head to think wealth, and sit their poor tails down somewhere". If we want to become people of wealth and not poor underclassmen any longer, we must seek out good strategies for storing "**Treasuries**", *where we shall lend to many, but borrow from none.* "*The wicked borrow with the intention not to pay back*" one way to combat borrowing our money is through promissory notes (legal IOU), professionally notarized with copies of two forms of I.D.; two current addresses; phone numbers, and filing fee with the probate court. This will slow down anyone from borrowing without being held liable. Our money is important to us, its for our families; and our living expenses. Remember to owe nobody, we don't have money to waste on foolishness. **Liabilities** are the burdens weighing down our potential wealth, but if we got to heap liabilities upon ourselves, do it as a corporate entity or a legal business. Companies with corporate contracts, accounts with corporate vendors, under our (EIN#); in this way we have potential wealth building strategies, and limited liabilities personally: this is the best potential for credit building, tax deductions, tax exemptions and acquisitions of assets. Gains will ensure debt equity (corporate bonds); convertible assets (preferred stocks), and potential equity in inventory, this can create potential cash flow; and with consistent earnings, we doing the kind of thinking make Wall Street come calling. So, now we understand the difference in making money moves, "**Assets**" are for the prudent (mature minds); and "**Liabilities**" are for the minors (immature minds). Stop letting someone else determine life worth for us, put away child's play, handle our money as mature adults do and our money decisions will increase our "Net Equity". For poverty is not an option; being poor is the decision to not seek educational tools for ourselves. Don't keep piling up debts or "**Red**" marks on our balance sheets. Learn, see, and hear the way to liberation, now!. For "**When In The Black**" our capital statements will establish leverage for us; for knowledge has no excuses, and knowing is half the battle, but defeating our opponents of useless debt and needless liabilities and other race groups having dominance over our money. Stay relentlessly focus on the pursuit of happiness; and keep our common focus on the keys to victories always lies "**When In The Black**". Asè.

Chapter 9.

Ninth: How to overcome negative losses in investing?,
A lost of anything we hold close to memory, is not easy to let go; but unless we dying alongside what we lost, life must go on in memory of the lost"... Once we read "Trading In The Zone" and "Becoming A Millionaire Real Estate Investors" and "New Market Wizard" and "The Richest Man In Babylon" and "A Random Walk Down Wall Street" and "The Power Of The Subconscious Mind" and "The Secret History Of The World" and so many others. We will see the key components to becoming a consistent winner in life; we must deal with the traumatic losses and the painful experiences in our hearts and minds; in which most was taught or acted upon us, especially when money is associated with the trauma. We can no longer operate in the emotional environment of not having enough, or something held us back, or we have no support; "**the power of attitude**" said "*if we say we can or can't, we are right*". For now on what we can do is operate in the "**courage to be rich**" don't let our fear of loss keep us from investing prudently in equitable people, places, things, and ideas. We must fund our future endeavors, we not getting younger again no matter what age we starting

from, it's not too late to take control of our emotional decisions about wealth. Ignore the stories that we grew with about the IRS for an example; see rumors have people afraid to become rich, due to tax fees and tax penalties on capital gains, but there are tax strategies that benefit the wealthy, get with wealth management companies, or expert CPAs, and experienced tax attorneys who know the loopholes we would need to maintain wealth. And apply these wealth management strategies to protect our investments. So in order to let go the past and "overcome" emotional fears (negative choices) today; that we inherited throughout our lives, many emotional choices we didn't self determine; we inherited them due to our mental environment. Lot of our parental teaching about money and the way we use it, begun in our homes; as it did in their parents houses. Many bad habits with money are due to lack of information and influence. Our parents lack of trading knowledge, and our personal perception about money over the years was the only thing we knew. We knew nothing on how "Investing" can benefit our future net worth and our personal challenges. This is why so many people working and hustling the hardest ways to get money; it's not the smartest ways of course. Creating money has very little to do with hard labor, and more so with our mental environment. Get rid of the fear of loss, it will hinder us from wealth or anything else worth pursuing... we will not experience "**Losses**" the same any longer; because all it take is the right winning attitude toward "investing" in ourselves, our communities, and our charities. For to obtain the wealth energy to work our plans we will have to be developed and plugged into the right mental channels. Reading these books, "Think and Grow Rich" and "The Law Of Success" and "Rich Dad, Poor Dad" and "Unleash The Power Within". My favorite "Green Power" and "The Black Titan" and "Black Wealth/White Wealth" and "Black Labor White Wealth" and "PowerNomics" help me to plug into the right mental environment and pursue education, and seek educated mentors to teach me about the steps to financial security, and teach me what an "**Asset**" truly is. Because of my definite of purpose I could tap into this energy, and experience how a first class lifestyle is afforded by the very few. The Robb Report magazine market to the true minorities who own and control all the wealth, they're the zero point zero one percent to the one percent wealth earners. These affluent groups hold all the wealth that's accumulated on the planet so far, so there's room still left to control some true wealth. Our billionaires and multi millionaires borrow from them in order to grow their visions in globally (aka *the new group of capitalist*), there's no such term as Self Made, perhaps Self Determine instead. But in researching deeper, I discovered that a good life can be attained around the five percentile to ten percentile income earners. We would need to generate one hundred and fifty thousand dollars or more a year without good investment strategies; that's a reachable goal, but I recommend we start now, finding expert brokers in **asset allocation**; while at the same time creating multiple streams of income to invest our money in for returns. Don't ever live life behind a paycheck, don't be putting "all our eggs in one basket" approach, that's a disaster waiting to bankrupt us. So let's get inside our mental environment and see how we spend our energy on senseless past emotions and fears of money. The keyword for now own is, "**Overcome**" the matrix of this word is a verb, when put in action, we *succeed in dealing with (a problem or difficulty). In order to get the better of, or prevail over until we control or bring under our control, or master intellectually, or defeat the opposition (the* *opponent); in this case, fears and failures with money*, but there are many other fears in our communities. The origin of the word came from old English to modern English diction (ofercuman, or over- come). The First translation were mention around the late 17th-18th century England. *See, to be over an estate, we must be ready to manage, protect, defeat, exceed what come our way.* I'm aware of a few passages to overcome loss, "those that walk and remain in perfect peace; keep their mind stayed on me"; and another, "our emotions and our memory may fail, but The Supreme Being is the strength of our memories and own wealthy portion forever, whom or what shall I fear'... Do not be overcome with anger when we lose a little amount of money in investing, that's just the portion of our money under risk in the markets, just manage our risk by overcoming our emotional attachment to money; we just risk whatever we able to invest, and keep educating ourselves and learn how to stay on course toward financial freedom". We can't be stressed over money, we must overcome the problems we created; by fixing our financial decisions, now! These are our personal challenges to wealth building, and can we solve these problems emotionally? and will we face them with honesty and realistic goals? Let's make the most of our income, and start taking small steps; this will be the key to our successes. Rid our minds of the negative past losses ancestrally, individually, and currently... Because a "**Negative**" mindset is the detriment to successful thinking. We learn from past experiences because the lessons are there to improve the present conditions in order to have a future. Every answer is in the past to better ourselves now, not to harp on it, and get all emotional, but to strengthen our resolves to build for our brighter tomorrow; in case today being our last to leave a legacy and an inheritance. So take a look inside the matrix of this word, and know how this word define our lives. "**Negative**" *is used as an adjective, which connotatively suggest the presence of distinguishing features either of a people, attitudes, or situations, or when something or someone not desirable or optimistic.* We can see inside this "**Negative**" *matrix as a noun as well; which are words or statements that expresses denial, disagreement, refusal, or rejection of a person, place, thing, or idea. The origin is Late Latin (negare, deny) to late Latin (negativus) to English (negate) to late middle English (negative);* mention around the late 17th century. A few wise saying about being positive:

"when the cares of our heart are many, our consolations cheer up our soul"; "keep our heart with all vigilance, for from it flow the springs of life"; "for the Supreme Being gave us a spirit not of fear but of power and love and self control". So to **"Overcome" "Negative"** thinking we must attack it, deal with it, conquer it; by simply using vigilance, awareness, self- determination, and intelligence. As life would have it, *"Losses" is much a fabric to wear; as the joy of winning is to self esteem"...* **"Losses"** are not always related to misfortunes, or negativity; sometimes a negative lose is gain. Gain of something or someone better. But in this case study, the matrix of this word **"Losses"** is the plural descriptive of the noun "Loss" which express *"the fact or process of losing something or someone". "Like insurance can protect us against financial loss"..* The origin of the word is old English (*los* or *destruction or breaking up*), this diction was first mentioned in the late 17th century. There too many examples of emotional losses in our families, and we probably experience them already, because we were not prudent with our money, we felt lost and abandoned when someone pass on and leave their love ones with debts, no money, and no insurance (this why the loss of a job due to new migrations and

downsizing is dangerous to our current wealth building; now we scrabbling for employment, afraid we going to lose stuff we worked paycheck to paycheck to purchase, all non liquid or depreciated inventory, and no **"liquid assets"** that we can convert immediately to cash to curve the loss of a job, migrations, and downsizing; we are now an emotional wreck until we find work. All because we were trained to go to school, get a job, save, retire, and travel; never taught entrepreneurship or to invest prudent money in different assets and asset classes, something we all need to obtain in the first place without going in the hole or in the **"Red"** for useless things we purchased and being held liable for; continuous liabilities, deficits, and debts piling up. That's why **"investing"** is the greatest tool to our potential freedom; you may ask what an investor look like, sound like, or talk like? look in the mirror, they look like us, sound like us, talk like us, but the question is, will it be us? See more than sixty-two percent of U.S. homes invest, but less than forty percent of black homes invest. Whites homes earns eight times more income than any other ethnicities in the U.S. For one simple reason; how do they perceive investing? The answer is far longer than five hundred plus years; they've been investing on behalf of their interest from the start of this new world explorations. They invested both short and long terms in order to own or control wealth for centuries; plain and simple. This kind of racial classism or group thinking have afforded many of their descendants early retirement plans far back as the thirteenth century through maritime trading with humans as their stocks, an "**Asset**" (read: "*The Case For Reparations-The Atlantic*") How many other ethnicities and their descendants enjoying the best centuries of their lives, because of what their ancestors chartered at the helm of their own financial ships.. See when acquiring "**assets**" and **asset Classes**, the majority of them are provided by people's labor; (a true fact). We can't operate a successful enterprise without people's labor; (cruel and unusual slavery is still an inhumane system of usury but laborers are assets) this why other ethnicities are seeking and providing a labor force for their own interest, first. So, "if we don't labor we want eat"; from the "**When In The Black**" investment strategies we become automatic investor" in order to slow down cruel laboring practices from other ethnicities who are doing business in their own best interest. So when we start up employment for ourselves to employ ourselves we will rise up to collect and seize the profits on our watch on our blocks; long before a great deal get away to another "investor" in our neighborhood who will gain profit from it, and hire his own race first, in which he should. He the creator of the jobs, it should be his right to hire laboring of his choosing, do we get the picture yet? People are corporate inventory, they are asset classes and sound equitable acquisitions (*people are liquid assets*). They can help with gains to cover losses. *"It's not personal, it's business"* So this why we invest in assets and asset classes to treat our employees justly, this how we show love, and provide decency and order to our social issues. **"When In The Black"**. Asè.

Chapters 10.

Tenth: How to be aware and avoid bad company?
"Associate *ourselves with people of good quality, for it is better to be alone than in bad company"... "For to make it at anything, we have to encourage ourselves to want the*

best"... For starters they're those who appear busy at doing nothing, but good actors at earning wages; contributing nothing on the clock, but to waste time and money. But let me ask who the company owner is; and the only answer we will get is; *"this job is for me to cash a check".* Now our companies filled with non productive; non innovative; non competitive; non interested employees who hinder their own personal growth, and income potential, therefore our companies stagnant, kept from becoming a leader in our industries. We need a team full of titans that will defeat the Gods if need be; champions exist as a winner within, self motivated, driven with passion; push themselves to be the best, and stay focus. We need to stay on top of our productivity, inventory, innovation and management teams. That mean focus our attention on both the micro level, and the macro level of managements, in order to increase the output performance of our companies, to gain handsome earnings in order to pay worthy employees beautiful salaries. All because we're organized as a proficient team, wanting the best results. I recommend such books as "Traction", "Scaling Up", "Four Hour Work Week" and "The Laws Of Success" to help us with innovation and to help streamline our stages of productivity for maximum participation and efficiency. Don't become extinct in our thinking, keep evolving with the times, this kind of thinking should come with those we add to our team to produce our set goals. A team with the right mental environment to compete and win in whatever industries we've chosen are trained not often hired. Remember when it come to our financial decisions in our companies; our motivation and focus must be family first, communities second; charities third, and our companies can make all these things possible. Of course whenever we have investments on the line, we can't bring in bad partnerships with different intentions or personal interest. We must protect the shareholders position in our decisions... must **"Avoid"** taking our companies down the wrong road by doing something illegal to make profits to meet bad partnerships greedy expectations. The same goals go for the associates outside our companies, we must discern who we congregate with, we must always be aware and avoid bad conversations about money, power, and wealth. it will corrupt our personal morals and our integrity as businesses. Honor our name and reputation above all else; we must learn trustworthiness with other people treasures early in our careers and lives; it will train us how to steward our own possessions, and our own power and our on wealth; but if we happen to be born with a wealth mentality at birth, and know how to become group made, and start our own businesses by flipping some products in demand, and risking money we invested, then go be group made right away. But this how to book are some things I paid dearly for, early in my life's lessons with my poor mentality. I didn't avoid the "*bad company*" advice, so that affected me in my decision making. I developed bad company or (a bad company) being loyal to people I grew to know over my young business years and felt a type of loyalty to them, even though it didn't benefit my vision or business at all, but I brought them in as business partners; and the wrong energy came with them, got my business under water with surveillance, and that eventually made me move from a great location; and things like that corrupted my good intentions and my good investments. So being "**Aware**", is the only choice we have when it come to losing all we envisioned. let's describe the word matrix of aware; this word as an adjective suggest *'most people are aware of the risk in investing, just not aware of managing their risk to invest'... See* "**Aware**" *is having* *knowledge or perception of a situation or fact. When we aware, we conscious of, mindful of, informed about, acquainted with, familiar with, alert to, checked out; especially potential advisers, friends, relatives, managers, employees, partners, and investors. Unless every person we know, or interviewed has elevated and developed their mental greatness, a catastrophe is inevitable.* Problematic situations will certainly happen in our life, and in our companies, but be vigilant, stay on our guard, and don't let it down one second. "**Avoid**" difficult people. Stay aware of our visions, and those we need to accomplish it with. We will rub people the wrong way, but best them than our vision. Vision combine with a good team can only enhance our dreams. Now that we learned to avoid certain things, be "**Aware**". The origin of the word **aware** is an old English word (*gewaer*); German word (*gewahr*); and modern English word (*ware*, or aware); first mention around the late 17th century. And we aware of the aggressive history of the 'New World' conquest and the visionaries behind it conceptualization; like these informative reads.

"*Christopher Columbus and the Doctrine of Discovery*", "*Tragedy and Hope (A History Of The World In Our Time)* " and "*The Anglo American Establishment*", in which we are all participants of until this very day. (The Cecil J. Rhodes Scholar Initiations) or "The Rhodes Scholars", they are scholarship supporters of Imperialism (A Great Britain Philosophy). But in spite of secret societies intentions; Americanism or Capitalism is one of the finest concept of any age in world history. Once the masses are aware of the six components of Americanism, and taught correctly to all who seek to learn; but remember these concepts are not taught to the underclassmen; this group equality and power will still be a personal choice for blacks, because group equality are obviously not the intention of the systems nor the leaders in the black communities. We must get busy by seeking out the mentors who've achieved their wealth goals as a group. See, what training we need and what training we are getting are two different matters to our advancing. But I can tell us definitively the black race group is at the lowest level of money knowledge. So we must avoid senseless money conversations, and mediocre goals about money, for wealth knowledge should be our goals. Don't expect other ethnicities or companies to choose us or to support us in becoming wealthy people, because we as a race group been taught to frown and speak ill of wealthy people, cutting off or cursing our wealth stream. Glad I didn't listen to such talk, but I sought out how they think; their mental capacity about power, and how the prudent perceive wealth as unlimited potential. To see the capabilities to control and own wealth comes from a place to thrive beyond surviving, where failure is not an option, and to return to a meager existence are not spoken of in their presence. This why their mental environment are attracted to "**Assets**". Their mental energy is wealth and they are brilliant investors, their minds are their assets. I learned this quote young "*I rather have one percent of a hundred men efforts, than one hundred percent of my own*"... So the gospel of wealth is associated with the interest of others efforts; for giving to the poor or the (mentally poor) is also great wealth advantages. Like: (Private Charitable Trusts); (Not For Profit Corporations) (Professional Sports Leagues)... For the wealthy (the mentally prudent), the IRS recognize up to twenty-seven different non profit corporations to use for federal, state, and local tax advantages, in other words giving charitable donations are for charitable deductions. Get with our CPA, Trust Attorney, and Investment experts on which not for profit corporations best suit our charitable endeavors. It's not a mean thing, it's a mental wealth thing. So in the meantime remember the tax system is designed to funnel vast amount of wealth to the few who give back, as long as we feels heroic to *'give back'*, these tax advantages and exemptions are being philanthropic advised, and I encourage using tax advantaged non profit corporations alongside, or hand in hand with our profitable corporations, and any prudent people or companies will continue to use what is available; these benefactors are known and used by the rich and wealthy magnate thinkers. So ask ourselves what class of thinking we privy to? and be honest about our influences, and see the people around us, and ask ourselves honestly, can they help us or hinder us from achieving our financial power. These people that influenced our lives are politicians, educators, pastors, advisers, parents, friends, relatives, associates, actors, musicians, celebrities, etc. If they're not mentoring us to accomplish our wealth goals, consider this thought; are they the problem then? And not just us, and are they using their powerless influences on us to hold us back by having us support them monetarily? Why do we have lack of money or lean purses, because they're unlearned as well, or looking out for themselves? Because we want a fat purse (lots of money) it is going to take powerful thinking, because rich magnates benefit from our poor thinking.. To "**Avoid**" *or to keep away from or stop oneself from doing (something); that benefit others only, we will need a mental overhaul.* "**Avoid**" is a verb, and the matrix mean we must take action. Like *avoid excessive liabilities to the death of us*; *like making the right decision to avoid or confront bad influences. The key to steering clear of, or staying away from bad company is;* making the necessary adjustments to avoid such incidents or people; or prevent poor thinking from happening in the first place. The origin of this word "**Avoid**" is old French (*vuide, empty*) to old French (*evuider, clear out, get rid of*) to English (*void*) to late middle English (*avoid*). *'This contract by law is nullified and void, therefore I avoid being liable by law'...* This word is late 17th century diction. Being "aware" of what the educational systems has cleared out from our minds about black history before slavery and after or how they 'avoid' teaching us that people were an asset and still is; when all we need is financial education, or our communities will be frozen as the permanent consumer class; (education will not teach us not to sign contracts with our signature on documents without parenthesis as doing business as); personal signatures are to be avoided at all cost as much as possible, and make sure it is a solid business contract; and we don't seek to fund our vision with others seed money first, like (pawn brokers, banks, hard lenders, venture capitalists). There are other avenues to startup something big; (like building businesses with family, friends, co workers, mentors, etc.). Getting credit and financial counseling certifications will help us as well. if we patient and get the education on how to avoid borrowing slave money, or purchasing depreciating inventory or non liquid items, we wan't convert our lives from mental poverty. We will need to stop with the personal liabilities, stop being the permanent consumer class. Purchase assets daily that accrue and compound interest. Borrowing money not necessary when we see each other as an "**Asset**". Now this conjunction, "**Bad Company**" *or failing to reach an acceptable standard or agreement with someone or with another company. We as group investors or companies can be an unfortunate union or can cause an unfavorable impression on others interested in our groups or companies.* I notice the word "**Bad**" was a redefine definition where I grew up, see, in the black community

'bad' can mean something favored psychologically; *like:*
'he bought a bad (good in our eyes debts) diamond rolex
watch, and it cost him several thousands dollars, boy he
must came into some money somewhere'... But in this
case study "Bad" is like: 'he risk all that money, on a bad
investment and now he can't recoup the money back, why
he bought a rolex watch, he could've done something else
with all that money". The matrix of '**Bad**' is often used as
an adjective, first known use of the word was around the
13th century old English (*baeddel, or baedan 'to defile')*
(sense of evil) (defective) (inferior) morally depraved
qualities.. I *am* reminded of a book called: *"And the*
crooked places made straight: The struggle for social
change in the 1960's. The American moment: Americans
never discussed or apologize for the history that occurred
and still relevant today, because they see it as business as
usual. When we look out on the broad landscape of social
equality in the workplace, in earning decent wages, and
antiquated curriculums, we need constitutional and
educational reform in our present conditions. Our society
is still intelligently bias at the core, fundamentally we
behind as a race group. What do I mean? if we would
listen to most ethnicities regardless of our current race

relations with other races, we still deeply segregated per capita. We often say, the "**Company**" *we network with, will determine our net worth. And "show me our friends, and I will show our future"; and "out of all the people we had to meet,* and *befriend, we met the con artist"*; but the matrix of this noun *is defined as a business or entity or fictional character* (but not necessarily a corporation in the United States.); *a legal entity made up of an association of people, be they natural to the land, Legal citizens, or a mixture of both, for carrying on a commercial or industrial enterprises.* The only way I can simply explain this definition. We are responsible for a "good company" or "bad company" literally. "The business of America Is business", and we are the United States companies; we are the United States balance sheets; we are account receivables and accounts payables, expenditures, expenses, exemptions, losses, gains, assets, liabilities, which summarize their GDP and their capital statements before the other nations. We are the full faith and credit of the United States. Call it invested interest, and the system of taxation keeps it going; if we the people fail to be free enterprises and a self determined nations. The beauty of Americanism is doomed. That's why I said be aware and avoid "**Bad Company**" because we are the companies... I Remember a quote; "I am not a businessman, I am a business. Man"... The origin of this English word "**company**" is found in an Old French military term *(compaignie), first mention in the middle 11th century, meaning a "body of soldiers" and from the late Latin (companio 'companion, one who eats with you")*. This book is written to help us see ourselves as companies of companions who I break bread with; of course that mean we must build ourselves as businesses by purchasing from each other companies large or small. Keep spending our currency with those we eat with the most. And that's entirely up to our definitive purpose, but our sole desire should be to stake majority of our resources as a race group on ourselves by bartering, purchasing or laboring for ourselves and trade with other race groups our goods and services. So, "**When In The Black**" our dollars are for individual investing and for the larger communities we eat with or go to battle with or (**we get money with**). So don't be associated with "**Bad Company**" giving our money to those who take food out our mouths; and give us garbage. If we are to be respected in the American dream as a free people; start being aware and avoid the toxic relationships with ourselves and the toxic business practices with ourselves. Leave all the naysayers behind when we building a successful vision, especially when we want our business relationships to last; we eat together, we get money together; we better together, "**When In The Black**". Asè

Chapter 11.

Eleventh: How to partner with the experts? "If we want to invest in some valuable asset classes, give our money to a janitorial engineer, instead of an financial adviser, see how far that get us". Positioning ourselves in the correct equitable partnerships will help us carry out our financial goals; or selecting the incorrect partnerships will carry out our money from underneath us... there are passages explaining this: "*for two are better than one, because they will be rewarded more for their labor*"; "*do not tie yourself up with a fool. For what partnership has wisdom with* *foolishness*"... Study the advantages in partnering with experts first, we simply need expert advice, it will be beneficial and profoundly efficient to spend our money on the best strategies. See, "*a person's gift makes space for him, and brings that person before powerful and influential people*"... But this passage is not necessarily talking about talents, skills or abilities. But instead how deeply in tune we are with the subconscious mind; or what prudent people call "**the Infinite Intelligence**" this is our first partner, let this voice within guide us to making great alliances with the correct experts. Some professionals are con artists who acquire degrees and licenses to operate simply on their own behalf, and can be the mastermind behind some recognizable ponzi schemes. Remember everything glitters isn't gold at the end of the rainbow. Many people have the gift to scam fools away from their money, but prudent people will ask hard question and investigate their legitimacy by seeking outside references, not from their references alone; and not from what their opulent lifestyles appear to be; another way is to secure a voucher to vouch people or companies; and before we partner with them, check their proper qualifications or expertise. Voucher's partnerships will secure us from potential loss, if the voucher highly recommend another company for their services, that can help insure our financial losses in case the people or companies not legitimate. Now look inside the matrix of this noun, "**Partner**". This word *is defined as a person who takes part in an undertaking with another or others, especially in a business or company venture with shared risks and profits. Someone we can collaborate with, colleagues with, associates with, teammates with, comrades with.* The origin of this word '**Partner**' come from Latin diction (*partitio, partition)* to Anglo Norman French (*parcener)* to *middle* English (*parcener, joint heir) to* English (*part, partner)*; to make sense of this term business wisely. (*it's a good idea to lay out specific terms at the outset, so that disagreements can be settled between the parties involved; whether it be with governments, nonprofits (501(c) companies, individual, or a combination of both, just say "**no, to my word is bond or handshake agreements**"*... Legal contract agreements are strongly preferred; such as general partnership (GP) or principal partner, silent partner, Limited liability partnership (LLP), Limited partnership (LP), or Publicly traded partnership (PTP) check your tax codes for each corporate structure.

Determine what goals best suit the alliance; Remember collaborating with individuals or company members is a unification of the minds in order to gain more assets and acquisitions. Another way to ensure a good working relationship are guaranteed payments to the "**Partner**" these payments to partners are payments that are to be made to a partner irrespective of whether the partnership makes a profit or not. These payments to partners are made to ensure that partners are compensated for specific contributions they make to a partnership, whether in the form of goods, services, or capital. This eliminates the risk of their making personal contributions of time or property for which they are never paid if the partnership is not successful. We only offer guaranteed payments to partners with the "expertise" we need. There many ways we can achieve our desired goals, through our "**expert network**" this is a group of accredited professionals who are paid for their specialized information and research services. **Experts** are commonly paid the high fees, it's associated with the provision of consulting services. Many may work under the **umbrella** of a larger company (Holdings or Parenting Company). Finding an all in one firm who can assist us with the majority of our startup needs would be great; we will need to control the: (EIN#, LLC, trademark, patent, copyrights, domain names, company website, 411 registry, 800#, business email addresses; business payroll, and business credit profiling (w/vendors) that report to Experian, Equifax, and Dun & Bradstreet for business credit. Buying these services are costly without a partnership agreement, but the inexpensive way for many of these steps to be accomplished will be done with patient filings ourselves; how you may ask? Consult an expert first if we have the capital, but if we don't follow these proven steps from my learnings; (remember just my opinion, I am not an accredited adviser, just my findings and experiences, just want to help… We can register and create our companies ourselves with patient applications. We can have our companies in a few minutes and on our way, and well within our spending habits. With the internet in our palms, we have access to the irs.gov; incfile.com; legalzoom.com; copyright.gov; godaddy.com (web host); shopify.com. (e-commerce host); tradeshownetwork.com (vendor accounts); 800.com; google.com/business; and we can report our vendor accounts to the three top corporate credit agencies I wrote of earlier, as our vendors accounts grows, our credit/cash limit will increase as well, and once we builded our relationships with the vendors, we will pay either net ninety, net sixty or net thirty day terms on our invoice accounts with a low cost rate per units or items. Remember seeking those with the expertise are to expedite the business startup process faster, and to expedite the unsecured credit lines faster; Now we understand the collaborations and intricacies of this word matrix as a noun or adjective. Soon we will become an "**Expert**" *a people who has a comprehensive and authoritative knowledge of something or the leading source in a particular area. A specialist, master, wizard, maestro, aficionado. When we get our amazing, talented, masterminds team it will expedite our successes.* The Latin origin of this word "**Expert**" is (*experiri, try*) to (*expertus*) to French (*expert*) to middle English (as an adjective) from French; and mentioned again in early 19th century, compared with experience and experiment. So the first experience and experiment will be to get these three experts in their area of expertise; we will need to partner with: 1. Certified Public Accountants 2. Trust Lawyers 3. Investment Management firms (my choice: **AV Financial**) Now after we reach and achieve the triangle of prudence or the pyramid of commerce protection; we on our way to becoming prudent businesses with the network needed, and the potential asset classes and asset acquisitions are within sight; with very few corporate liabilities (debt obligations) we on our way to wealth accumulation. And with seasonal growth we'll soon learn (convertible stocks and corporate bonds), these can generate income as an option to help curve expenses). When building successful and sustainable companies, our visions must be executed on schedule if possible; and remain focus on the business plans as stated; wisely and precisely with a definitive purpose, and with a burning desire to achieve our greatness together as a team. And with the earlier chapters guiding us; we will notice quickly the steps to achieving, **"When In The Black"**. See we becoming great partners of commerce exchange and with mercantile we will increase everyone in our wealth zone, all our experts and networks will have net worth and all our endeavors will manifest wealth for the good of all people, especially **"When In The Black"**. Asè.

Chapter 12.

Twelfth: How to live, When In The Black: *"only as one people, one aim, one destiny. For wealth and worth are these, "when we come to know a healthy portion of all we earn are ours to keep"*...and *"when we are **Masters** of our destiny, free to take or reject at will, we take the power, we take the wisdom, shine as a light among the children of men, we don't be high-minded in our wisdom; dialogue with the ignorant, as well as the wise, and be true to ourselves"*... It's a privilege to be *in the black*; we now know our purpose for writing this book; it is to ignite our mental wealth strategies for all people's equality, but starting with ourselves. To invoke progressive positive implementations for acquiring assets and investments that can improve our social, economical, political, financial, educational, governmental systems against blacks in these competitive markets. I'm here writing this book for the equal elevation of the black race and their group economics first, in order to enter the free market system of capitalism called Americanism. We must compete for real wealth, power, worth and influence in the market; and so to tackle this daunting task of eradicating the emotional environments of poor thinking and the mental baggages that keep our race disconnected, the lacking of trust in our race have us living in failed communities; this psyche is not beyond remedy, but we running out of excuses as long as we still blaming others for something we can do for ourselves; no other race will respect our laziness, lack of commerce, failure of development; so when and where did we inherit this non competitive posture? We must quit being participants in the biggest brainwashing exhibitions on the black minds by our own black leaders ever carried out, to keep black wealth white wealth. And the Sunday services need to be held accountable for storing up our hard earned cash in our communities and ignoring the economic deprivation in our neighborhoods which is the main cause of crime; for the cruel and unusual punishments our black children experiencing are unconstitutional; they are being unconstitutionally violated and not given equal protection and due process provisions under the Constitution, they are incarcerated with adult prisoners to be violated mentally and physically; and all these horrible mental symptoms inherited by our people are due also to the high unemployment rate in our own neighborhoods, why? Because we want other race groups to hire us before their own race do. Where are the black owned construction companies, design firms, corporate franchises, schools, hospitals, grocery stores, loaning institutions that we need to build a health environment in our communities? We need to create jobs for our kids, for this will help levitate crimes our people committing on each other. Here's a passage we've all heard in Sunday services, "*the world (others outside our group) loves his own. And if we belonged to world (the other groups) it would love us as it own, but I have chosen you people out (of the other groups) the world. That's why the world (the other groups) hates you". *(All groups has this mental competition instinctively, as pointed out in the written scripts)*. But we still got beliefs in something gonna change if we wait, for no other race wait on fate, should black people? "**Faith without works, is dead**"*... Invest in ourselves, we can employ and compensate ourselves through the shifting of our "**mental wealth and mental security**" stop begging and complaining and get in the monopoly game of life, we in the wizard of Oz, we in the American dream, and because of our dependent minded leaders and our own poor thinking dependency as well, we will keep empowering other groups to keep us bond by inequalities. It's a lucrative business, to keep the status quo the same, its nothing emotional about doing business, we are allowing ourselves to becoming domicile to a third class citizenship as of now, and dropping by the years. Our ancestors were the wealth builders for different European countries, and this home nation, and now over six hundred years later the only shift of wealth is our black dollars are the cornerstone of consumerism for the entire globe. Because of the economic mental problems we continue to endure, at our own doing, some say its because of the past mental traumas of slavery brought forward in our own psyche, in which some can be traced to the past, but now we clinging to those excuses why we can't do great exploits without integration or inclusion. Many still spend unproductive time debating about what race superior over the other, when the only race to win is with power, wealth and worth. These are the determining factors to equality; for no race can be powerful or prosperous without doing commerce first and the best, and acquiring a labor force to put their plans in action. We still manage money, developing land and utilizing resources different as a race group, but this mentality came from inside and outside influences on our psyche; we can't continue these psychological wars on our mental worth, therefore it has affected our mental wealth. Can we see the mental games played can take the straight or crooked paths to poverty, if we waiting for someone to help us, good luck. See fairness is a place where they judge pigs, and we know the outcome of that, they go to the slaughter house. So whatever direction a system takes us, this how to book will make it all a competition, by being competitive in three ways with other ethnic groups, compete by purchasing our own assets, laboring for our own assets, or bartering our own assets. And if we don't compete we will stay in these four categories: borrowers, laborers, consumers and criminals. As a race group we becoming the permanent underclassmen (beggars and criminals). See what will continue to happen if other groups don't hire us we'll become expenses, expenditures, liabilities, and exemptions, and what will that give us, a free go to prison number and below minimum wage work (the thirteenth amendment) or genocide; this will be our reward black people. With this book being on course with the historical wealth path of the past, a change can only come at the hands and minds of the bold. Its my intention and interest to award the readers with the badge of wealth. "**When In The Black**"... can take our communities on a courageous ride to be wealthy, worthy and working to keep us **in the black.** For throughout the ages it took unwavering courage to see generational wealth while under extreme conditions and extreme prejudices; far over thousands of years our ancestors advanced civilizations for many to envied tip this day, for the black people's contributions alongside all other races were to further and better humanity way of life. History must recognize and record the contributions from people of all ethnicities; but the hidden figures "**in the black**" in totality are beyond priceless, uncountable, and undervalued. We are worth our price of admission so lets give thanks to our indigenous ancient ancestors and present ancestors for going beyond the call of life to thrive against all odds and still rise, this why I still rise, this why we all still rise. (We wealth defining) but stop giving our wealth away, "**When In The Black**"... You can see when individuals or corporations need to get out of the "**Red" they use the term "in the black"** as the material descriptive of a positive balance or surplus on a company financial statements; **like 'black Friday' in November,** which indicate the coming of the end of a business cycle, a summary of the fiscal year before tax season. So their marketing campaigns to get out the hole or out of the **"Red"** is associated with profit, for every dollars helps with wall street calculations, shareholders profits and executives bonuses. This the best psychological advantage I have ever learned about in business. They cater to their permanent consumer class, it's just brilliant business as usual. (*Black people money must cease from being other's wealth*). Therefore companies are said to be **"in the black"** when it is profitable or when the company produces positive earnings after accounting for all expenses. The same applications are needed in our personal challenges to change this mental paradigm from poverty, such as accountability, balanced budgets, and positive earnings, when we all become business minded and take nothing personal or emotional like our opponents, we'll create a life free of mental poverty and a life free of emotional baggages that attempting to claim our full potential to be divinely powerful and competitive people in the race for power, wealth and worth. See all we say and do should be to rise, compete, and advance our cause and effect on society, without being oppressive to people; it's smart to build self esteem, in order to protect our investments, we want to be competitive, and we want to create jobs for us and other ethnicities too. See, this saying "**in the Black**" is positive and prosperous. Black is often used in an adjective matrix in a connotative way, the origin is ancient, but resurface under Germanic observation during the 18th century perspective in Europe; not denoting a noun or a verb in this matrix. The term '**in the Black**" can cover a wide range of subjectivity; it can cover non material and material meanings; this word to date is fairly young in a etymological sense of (**Kush/ Kamit**), but will forever be utter in the annals of times for many things… see the latest version of the word "**black**" go back to old English (*blaec, black*); remember it first mentioned again in the early 18th century Germanic. See Europe went through the Moorish conquest, dark age, black plague, and famines for several hundred years; and they associated all their emotional trails to this word, by describing it emotionally they lost all empathy for the sake of survival and these dark conditions are what set their voyage to the new world without mercy and cold hearts; and along with the Pope's christian decrees, one was called *the doctrine of discovery: The political and religious conversion of all non christians people around the world which launched the land removals acts of Africa and America..* But in this how to book **"When In The Black"** is not only about racial inequalities or any other adjective on racial injustice. It's a tutorial to self directing our money or to guide us to wealth management that change these mental and material conditions; and through seeking accredited advice and expertise from a wealth perspectives no matter the teacher's color, learn. This book is the **"Asset"** guide, it's about not owing money, unless for profitable returns, *"in other words, we managed to stay **in the black"**.* We consistently remain **"debt-free", in credit, in means, financially sound, paid liabilities, creditworthy;** making sure our companies nor our individual financial statements never end up in the **"red"**, because in all our getting from this asset guide, we get understanding on how we receive mental wealth, and how to obtain our mental security. Knowing **"Security"** is a class of stocks that give us equity ownership in companies, and through prudent investigations and diversified investments in *"**Assets**"* only; we will win our piece of the wealth pie. Avoid these race wars, they just mental distractions to subjugate us to reverse racism, which is not possible, we as a black race group can't substantially change nothing under the white power structure, we own nor control nothing of significance; our disconnected wealth can not challenge any world power to demand equality, because as of now, we control nothing in no governmental way. They have as of now the dominion over the majority of wealth, power and influence to affect our race through legislative systems; whether it be socioeconomic, political or governmental. Why get involved in such foolishness? When **assets and asset classes** are publicly accessible, the answer is right in plain sight, but the black race are trained and programmed to choose debt obligations and contractual liabilities agreements, (purchasing bad depreciating debt); and tricked to sign temporary contract called bill of rights. But when we finally become mentally free to create opportunities, supply a market, be of demand, be innovative, partnering with industry titans, networking with experts, being charitable, helping humanity, and give the world our *"surety of wealth"*, so all races can profits from our above the ground **black market** as well, we will be in the right race to worth, wealth and power as a race. I am here to give my portion and give my life's worth for a more abundant outcome, to see our cup overflow, run over with wealth strategies to keep pouring out upon our families forever. Keep listening to our infinite intelligence within for our wealth shift by revisiting "**How to live, When In The Black**", we must master our equity position and our net worth by loving ourselves first, as well as our neighbors. Remember: **Assets - Liabilities = Black Net**... So **when in the black** our family lives are improving, we live free to create and generate true wealth, and maturely oversee our estates and manage our own affairs. Constantly masterminding our visions, bringing together experts, partners, investors, and networks to determine our net worth, while remaining charitable to humanity through prudent investments. Stop letting everyone benefit reversely but us "**When in the black**". is all about us first in our communities, lets eat together in love. For We too are the people of Americanism·and can't go backward to a meager existence in which our ancestors paid a horrible price, because we know the wealth road to freedom is in our definite, precise, and accurate purpose; because in our group purpose we not into heaping trillion of dollars for purchasing material things only, that's not why we are *competing in this race for wealth. We Looking to compete against other race groups at doing business and commerce; so we like them can express our power, wealth and worth as a people too. So stop trying to make "the powers that be" to repent for implementing so much bondage on our race, it want happen; we must correct our own emotional environment within by saying, "I haven't gotten in the way of wealth thinking, for it is a sin, if I limit God". Say, "I am Creator of more than enough".* We are enough. See this book is written to inspire mental wealth because of the past forty plus years of failures and successes; observations, and participations in the politics of Americanism. And with much selective thoughts from reading, researching and **applying principal wealth strategies,** I desired to become one of great citizens of wealth on the planet as well; yes emulating what the past and present prudent men and women did implement to win at wealth thinking, *because someone has to think and provide for the poor minded thinkers under a capitalist system.* These rich wealthy magnate thinkers give and yield resources during and after their life's on earth in their own unique ways. And the common thread that connected the rich thinkers with the poor thinkers is this;

Stewardship. it's simplicity amazed me, because the masses or majority are driven by a different applications and executions of money; or a lack of stewardship for humanity, and the few rich wealthy magnate thinkers must rule over the poor impoverished thinkers. They do not share systemically the same information about money to them to remain at the top all because they believe they are better steward of money. These very smart groups strategically ensure collective superiority over individualism. See collectively the privy want share their interest or information about the right way to invest in assets and asset classes, because it not lucrative business to teach the permanent consumer class anything, for nothing emotional about that, its business as usual. And blacks are very emotional, entitled and stubborn; when all we need is courage, and assertiveness, and will to compete. The problem we must solve in our minds is to stop letting others call us a lazy group of people. That's reverse psychology, Capitalism is a concept in which we don't work for ourselves, but getting others to work for us to extract resources and wealth to give to us. This how six hundred plus years of nearly free labor acquired generational wealth for the Europeans. So much wealth for one race during and after the fourteenth century until now. See once upon a time, blacks in this country was not considered a class at all, until the Emancipation Proclamation of eighteen sixty-five, and the second Constitutional amendment. Whites had to work their own land for the first time since the migration from Europe, because black laborers left the lands and begin to do for themselves, but the south wouldn't let us go and grow, so our wealth progress remain slow and many had to transfer to the industrial plants of racial inequalities. Still only a few hundred thousand blacks were semi free out of four million during the Reconstruction era of terror; we saw some political and economical progress to easily be snatched away, all its progress and resources confiscated under Jim Crow segregation, Eminent domain and others. And after the separating of the two races systemically, we actually owned, controlled, and builded counties, cities, and states alongside natives and whites who once owned blacks as well. See the details on "The Trail Of Tears"... And now these other ethnic groups migrating into the United States again to removed us from the labor force and commerce opportunities because of our failures to develop as a race group... This socioeconomic, political annihilation through migrations on blacks settlers started long ago, around late eighteenth and nineteenth century under President William McKinley and his successor Theodore Roosevelt when they allowed many struggling migrants from Europe to be shipped here on the ports of America to assist them in **the American Dream** slogans in Europe. Now many race groups becoming a force in Americanism again and will soon push more black people into the unemployment lines. That's why daca was designed for while under President Barack Obama administration but now under attack by the current President, to slow down the migration of the hispanics into the American dream, so they want take white people jobs, "to make old America great again" is the aim on his mind... But if we don't use group economics, and political lobbying to progress in the wealth pie, we as a race group will be doomed to the underclassmen status, I don't want that for our children who left behind to struggle in the future for the equality we should give them through our group effort to create worth, wealth and power. But many other migrant race groups are here to get their piece of the wealth pie in the commerce world, which afford them real status and respect. And all these groups build their wealth from the consumer class (mostly black people). Even when researching over the years for the wealthiest information in various ways, there are still many hidden strategies to unlock these secrets, they were passed down throughout history to the privy only. I didn't discover a step by step instructional guide on how to correct the mental environment in such poor impoverished thinking. I just shifted my own mental wealth; found no new magical life changing information on how to correct people from a struggling mindset, or a magical potion to become one who have the wealthiest ambition; after reading the thousands of watered down versions on how to do books everywhere. I came to this conclusion; it's our mental environment that we inherited from our parents experiences, not all experiences of our own choosing, nor consent. But "parental advisory suggested" or the lack of suggestions about wealth, our minds must be transformed individually or collectively in order to advance as wealthy, worthy, productive people. **So *what is the meaning of life without mental wealth? An unfulfilled life*,** and we know people as individuals and as groups who have achieved mental worth and wealth by working their mental energy toward collective success. But this book is especially for black people who can also find these treasures mentally as well. Listen nobody holding us back from wealth and worth but our disconnected Black People with attitudes toward each other. See the magic is in our definitive purpose; listen, a definite of purpose with a burning desire and a driven passion will bring freedom to pursue and compete for our families, communities, and charities. So I suspend my ending with this passage, "I desire above all else, we prosper and be of health, even as our soul prospers *(our conscious and subconscious minds are one going forward)* (living wealthy lives)... Remember **"When In The Black"** prosperity is a lot easier when we unite to own and control our portion of the resources, wealth and power in every nation. Love you all. Asè.

About the Author

Daryl D. Jones, Sr. was born in 1967, in Jefferson County, Alabama. A resident of Smithfield in Birmingham, Alabama, as a youth he was gifted with a advance mind, and advance talents. And he worked his gifts in the community he grew up in and earned money at an early age by barbering, drawing, painting, and tutoring. Also made money throwing newspaper routes, helping the elderly around grocery stores, and selling merchandising. Mr. Jones is a graduate of Ensley High School, and Lawson State Community College, he also attended Booker T. Washington Business College, and Miles College for finance and accounting. He open his first business in 1992, at twenty-five years old in the downtown business district of Ensley, Alabama. He the proud father of two sons, he preached his first sermon on "The Christian Empire" from the gospel as a youth minister at (The Guiding Light Church) under the Honorable Bishop James L. Lowe, Jr., he impacted countless lives on the dangerous street corners, where he was once a member of the same hard knock life.

Mr. Jones is a business advisor, investor, motivational speaker, author, and advocate of the ancient african spiritual systems, and a loving friend; he enjoys reading, researching and planning business projects. He love helping people prosper with their health and their money. For more information or to contact

Mr. Jones email him wealth@theblacktitangroup.net Thank you for supporting this book of wealth, and may it richly advance us all. Asè.

The Black Titan Publication (c) ™

Made in the USA
Columbia, SC
27 January 2018